My Tapestry of Life

Spiritual and Friendship
threads forever woven
into my Tapestry.
Relax with time.
Enjoy my rhyme.

Linda Messel Potter

May 2021

My Tapestry of Life

Celebration Poems and Rhyming Stories

LINDA MESSEL POTTER

lpacademy47@gmail.com

Library of Congress Control Number: 2020923876
ISBN: Hardcover   978-1-6641-4464-4
                     Softcover   978-1-6641-4463-7
                     eBook   978-1-6641-4462-0

Rev. date: 01/07/2021

To order additional copies of this book, contact:
Xlibris
844-714-8691
www.Xlibris.com
Orders@Xlibris.com
817422

Contents

BIRTHDAY THREADS
Husband And Wife

BIRTHDAY THREADS
Daughters
Sons-by-Marriage

BIRTHDAY THREADS
Grandchildren

BIRTHDAY THREADS
Family And Friends

CHURCH AND BIBLE STUDY THREADS

GET WELL THREADS

GRADUATION THREADS

HERITAGE THREADS

HOLIDAY THREADS

POTPOURRI THREADS

SYMPATHY THREADS

TEACHING SCHOOL THREADS

TRAVEL THREADS

TRIBUTE THREADS

A Tapestry

That's what my life seems to be.
Moving ten times during my married life,
Trying to be a nurturing mother and supportive wife.
Always picking up and continuing the threads,
Being woven into various patterns in my heart and head.
Threads of church, friends, and family,
Of activities to keep us strong and healthy.
My poems have become the threads
Telling life stories from my heart and head.
They represent the times I wanted people to know
I took the time to make a rhyme, my caring to show.
And from the start so long ago
Could I have known the design to be so?
Yet the Tapestry continues to change
As life never remains the same.
So many choices of threads over time.
Before you my tapestry, my reason, my rhyme.

When you read, may you see
The deep love for my family.
The ups and downs of daily life,
The hope and healing from strife.
The laughter and tears,
The faith that calmed fears.

May my Tapestry inspire each one of you
As you live and create your own unique design, too.
Choices, memories, beliefs, the threads you weave,
Your own special Tapestry to achieve.
Choose wisely how you weave your tapestry,
So one day you will be pleased with what you see.

Tapestry Threads

Anniversary Threads, husband, wife,
Love, Silver, Golden Threads for life.
Rainbow Colors, Sea Glass Fibers,
Tested over time, kinder, wiser, finer.

Colorful Cotton Birthday Threads,
Cotton is strong, supportive, it is said.
Church Threads of Strong Nylon or Polyester,
Faith, worship, prayer, praising for sure.

Warm, Soft Woolen Threads, Get Well Soon!
Feel my compassion, heal your wound.
Graduation Threads, Mohair feels light.
Fly to your dreams day and night.

Grandchildren Threads, Sparkle Yarn Fibers
Bring enjoyment, pleasure, new event glitters.
Heritage Threads of Regal Silk, the finest.
Our love and admiration, the highest.

Holiday Threads, various brilliant Sea Glass Fibers.
Vibrant colors for different holiday flavors.
Potpourri Threads, interesting mix of surprise.
The pattern and design begin to arise.

Sympathy Threads, Boucle yarn fibers, soft and light,
Reflection, loss, tears, need comfort tonight.
Teaching Threads, Acrylic fibers, wide range of colors.
Wide range of students, reading, writing, numbers.
Exploring, experimenting, learning,
Problem solving, thinking, achieving.

Travel Threads of Colorful Ribbon fun,
Exploring new places, maybe in the sun.
Tribute Threads of gold and silk beauty,
Going beyond the call of duty.
All my poems could fit this Tribute file.
Each person's thread going the extra mile.
Always bringing to mind a smile.
Living life with one's own style.

Dedicated To

My husband, who is the first person to listen to what I have written and edit my poetry with his keen ability to spot errors. He has, for many years, encouraged me to publish my poems and share my gift for rhyming. His excitement for each poem always encourages me. He also understands, when I have an inspiration, I need whatever time it takes to complete the poem. He loves sharing that many of those inspirations are written on a napkin, paper towel, or whatever scrap of paper is near at hand. I swim laps for exercise, and have been known to exit the pool, dripping wet, to record my rhyming thoughts before continuing my swim.

My family, and *friends,* whose enjoyment and praise of my poems, encourages my continued rhyming. For some, the only poems received have been from me. For others, they cannot believe I actually wrote a poem just for them. My pleasure comes from reading my poem out loud to each person and seeing their excitement and response.

My grandchildren, who post my poems on their bulletin boards and look forward to the poems I write for their special celebrations and events. Because they think my poetry is amazing, I keep writing.

My Mother, Phyllis Messel, who played rhyming games with our family during long, vacation trips in the car. Maybe my enjoyment in rhyming began in those early childhood years. After my Mother's death, I discovered many poems she had written. Looks like poets run in our family.

Thank You To

My husband Ron, who, throughout the years, has encouraged me to write more poems and self-publish. He's the first to hear my latest poem, search for corrections, be amazed at what I have created, and ask why I don't publish. Our fifty-plus years of marriage have woven an amazing, beautiful, interesting, tapestry, inspiring many of my poems.

My family and friends, who adore the poems written about them, complement my rhyming, and encouraged my publishing. It is your life threads that have become part of my tapestry and inspire my writing. The joy for me comes in reading my poems out loud to each of you and watching your reaction of joy, laughter, and excitement.

My friend, Jan Miller, who saw my thick poetry binder, read some of my poems, insisted on my ability to move forward and introduced me to her published sister. Jan set us up on a lunch date, drove me to Venice to meet her sister, spent the day with us, and drove me home. She gave me Barbara Feltquate's poetry book, *Silhouettes of Life*, showing me that her poems were similar to what I had written. Confidence began to grow, but when would I find the time? Then six months later, COVID-19 quarantine supplied plenty of *at home time* to write and create My *Tapestry of Life*. Maybe something positive could come from this challenging period in time.

Poet Barbara Feltquate, who explained the publishing process, calmed my fears, and encouraged me to use her publisher. She was always there to answer questions as I proceeded. Jan's and Barb's excitement sealed the deal.

My Granddaughter Shelby Storm and friend Kerry Bidle who taught me the necessary computer skills for the task. Not being an easy assignment, both of you were very patient and kind, understanding, and still as close as my cell phone.

Anniversary Threads

Create my tapestry,

Written here for all to see.

Ron and Linda

I share these poems, recount my life.
Married to Ron, fifty-plus years, his wife.
His need for two heart valves nearly ended our run.
Made us rethink our life. Would there be time for more fun?
Surgeries, recovery, blessings abound.
Have fun reading about our ups and downs.

Celebration Dinner

November 5, 1988 is the day.
Celebration Dinner is the way.

Twentieth Wedding Anniversary is the reason.
For Ron Potter and Linda, it was the season.

Beginning at six p.m., Bride and Groom aren't late.
Please bring a dish to share. We'll provide the plate.

Bring a wedding photo. We thought it would be fun,
To share those special pictures with everyone.

Share a story surrounding your wedding time,
A fond memory, unexpected event, or rhyme.

Please RSVP so the Bride and Groom,
Will know how much wedding cake you will consume.

Phone 805-499-1558
We hope you can keep this date.

Nine two three Deer Spring Place, Newbury Park.
Why not wear your wedding veil for a lark?

Memories That Never Fade Away

Twenty-five years we celebrate today.
July, 1967 Louisville, Kentucky It all started on that first blind date.
Where we were the night you asked me to be your mate.
Running in from outfield in Jiffy uniform and socks.
The many trips I made to visit you at Fort Knox.
Ready for work at Fireman's Fund in your green suit with briefcase.
In your hat singing carols in our VW, that special look on your face.
Walking through corn fields, watching city lights,
Trying to be together most every night.
Duck races and picnics by the lake with the big tree,
Showing off my engagement ring to friends and family.

November 16, 1968 I love you, you said,
raising my veil, kissing your bride.
Kneeling during the Lord's Prayer knowing
you'd always be by my side.
That champagne cork, pizza, honeymooning at the Hotel Brown,
Wondering if my grandfather was working late and still around.
Our first apartment, 1264 Cherokee Road, by the park,
Granny Kanzler falling into the clothes
basket—was the room too dark?
That Friday, December 13, 1968, you left for Vietnam.
Away for six months to serve Uncle Sam.

Six months later, Friday the thirteenth, became our lucky day.
June 13, 1969 You returned safely home to stay.
Tapes, letters, photos, and prayers got us through
A very hard separation time, for us two.

That embrace at the airport, a new
apartment, *3010 Hikes Lane*, to see.
Furniture, wedding presents, how great married life was going to be.
Me getting ready for you to come home from work every day.
How cooking dinner and cuddle time were my own special way.
A trip to San Francisco to begin our vacation log.
Golden Gate Bridge, Sequoias, Tea Garden, Monterey, and fog.

The call to say, *You're going to be a Dad.*
You in side burns when it was the fad.
A rocking chair you sanded and stained.
The yule log you made that will always remain.
Trips to Covered Bridge, French Lick, and Florida's Destin Beach.
February, 1972 That first house at *4908*
Ulrich Road, a new goal to reach.
Calling you at the ball park to say, *Hurry home, Dear.*
Time to go to the hospital. Our baby's arrival is near.
Your indecision about what to wear that night.
Coaching me through natural childbirth so I'd do it right.

June 23, 1972 Overwhelming tears of joy
at the birth of our first child.
Little *Miss Jennifer Renee*, so gentle and mild.
The roses you sent, the drive home full of caution and care.
The love relationship the three of us would share with *Mr. Pooh Bear.*
So many wonderful firsts I could never rename them all,
But our life with Miss Jennifer has been filled with love, joy, and awe.

October 11, 1974 Then two years later, the birth of *Miss Jill Marie.*
She was strong and aggressive; we could all see.
Remember the pull-ups you did with her in our bed,
While she was yet so tiny, not much hair on her head.
You and I taking turns patting her to sleep at night.
Her cuddling up to *Bunkie* to calm a fright.
Gym team, diving, volleyball, and track.

3

Your coaching made each sport a little easier to hack.
Jill's energy level was always on high,
Like trying to catch a moonbeam or star in the sky.
Her loving, loyal, caring ways
Have given us many special days.
Family celebrations, Couples' Club fun,
Cards with the Bunnells, Jiffy ball games won.

June, 1977 Our first move away, would
Minnetonka, Minnesota be right?
You saw the house at *18801 Hanus Road*
and said, *We'll take it tonight.*
The flowers you cut from the garden for me.
A snake you found, while cutting grass, for all to see.
The horse who ate our bushes in the snow.
Skiing and snowmobiling when it was fifty degrees below zero.
The four of us biking down that long hill
And Jill holding on to avoid a spill.
Duck hunting trips and Adrian fun.
Working the garden, photographing our yield in the sun.
The bird on your head, ball games to play.
My piano, your ball team helped move in, that first day.

October, 1979 Our move to *2555 Toltec Circle in San Ramon*,
Far away, but not so alone.
Bartlett, Snage, Malkmus, Cannon fun.
Picking out our Christmas tree in the *California* sun.
Hours spent assembling a Barbie Doll
House for Christmas surprise.
The delight and gleam in both daughters' eyes.
A five-foot-six Bunny arriving on Easter Day.
The earthquake that happened while you were away.

June, 1980 The move to *Indianapolis,*
Indiana, 7601 Noel Forest Lane

An acre of land and heavy woods we would gain.
Remember asking, *When the ladies see*
this house, what will they say?
You choosing the radio jam box (instead of
new golf clubs) for Jen's birthday.
Planting our yard with grass seed, flowers, and one hundred trees.
Trips to Disney World, Sea World, and Washington, D.C.
You appearing at the swimming pool fence after golf to say, *Hi.*
Watching us swim and dive and be anything but dry.
Indianapolis was the beginning of our bird-watching days.
Doves, Finches, Chickadees, and unusual Nuthatch ways.
Learned how to be tennis partners, make the matches fun.
I often rode my bike while you trained to run.
In all my volunteering time, you supported me.
At church, school, scouts, Bible Study Fellowship, working for free.
We gained pleasure from watching our ladies do their thing:
Piano, cello, scouts, gymnastics, ballet, swimming, diving, choir sing.
Stacking wood for fires in the fall.
Grandfather clock chiming in the hall.
Pool table fun and Eagle Creek Park.
Home-made ice cream at the wood's edge before it got dark.
Winter sledding on that big snowy hill.
Longworths, Johnsons, good memories still.

October, 1984 923 Deer Spring Place, does that ring a bell?
Back to *California, Newbury Park* this time, oh well.
Azaleas, Roses, and all kinds of flowering trees.
Bougainvillea, Carnations so beautiful to see.
Grapefruits, oranges, lemons too.
Strawberries, guava, always something new.
Our yard was a blooming delight.
Sunshine from morning until night.

We could go to the beach, twelve months of the year.
See the mountains that were always so near.

Tennis and running, we did it all.
We were never at home. Don't bother to call.

In October we got Molly for Jill's thirteenth birthday surprise.
Remember the happiness in her eyes.
Molly's first trip to the beach at Point Mugu.
Posing for a Christmas card shot, sitting on the rocks, too.
Santa Barbara trips, eating shrimp and fish on the pier.
Arts, crafts, beach volleyball, sailboats,
mountains, sunshine, it's all here.
Vacations to Maui, snorkeling fun.
Fishes, flowers, beaches, and sun.
Easter Sunrise Service, black lava beach.
The Plantation, Lahina, and golf all in reach.
That special trip to Solvang to purchase my ring.
Disney, Catalina, Hearst Castle trips of which we sing.
Falling asleep at Point Mugu one Sunday afternoon.
Waves lapping at our towel, waking us none too soon.
Pastor Lawson, Fiores, Westlake Church friends.
Bartletts, Van Arsdales, Hesses, memories to the end.
Watching the metamorphosis from little
girls to young ladies, take place.
Always seeing Jennifer and Jill with a tan on their face.
Boys, braces, cheerleading fun.
A football kidnap party in the sun.
It was while living here, we both turned forty!
We gave each other a great surprise party.

January, 1989 Another move, to the Midwest we've come back.
Our yellow rental house in Naperville, Illinois, at 910 Lilac.
Taking you each day to the Naperville train.
Picking you up in the Kiss and Ride lane.
Watching the building progress of our house each day
At 4018 Broadmoor Circle, make way.
Landscaping, flowers, another tree,

Making our yard the way we always wanted it to be.
Wallpaper, drapes, furniture new.
Special touches for the inside, too.
Family and friends to share new home joy.
A riding lawnmower, your latest toy.
Watching Arnold Palmer on opening day.
If you love golf, White Eagle Country Club's the way.
Golf rounds, tournaments, prizes, and trophies won.
You certainly are an awesome golfer, Hon.

Runner up for the Club Championship.
I love your swing; the way you turn your hip.
Memories of our ladies' busy high school years
With all the trials of growing pain tears.

Homecomings, proms, and Valentine dances,
Track and volleyball team chances.
Attempts at trying to make it to state.
The telephone busy until very late.
Friends always around to sleep and eat.
Friends always around were really a treat.
The phone always busy with calls coming in.
The house was always in a spin.
Vacationing in San Destin, Phoenix, Disney, and Epcot.
Coming home from Dallas, finding it anything but hot.
Time spent at the River Walk.
Late at night when we lay and talk.
Garden plots and biking fun.
Taking our Golden Retriever, Miss Molly, for a run.
Spring time flowers in full bloom.
Planting summer flowers until there's no room.
Colors of Midwest fall leaves aglow.
Winter skiing and walks in the snow.
Sunset colors or planes overhead.
Birds from all over Illinois waiting to be fed.

Mexican food at Potter's Place, movie time.
All five clocks set and ready to chime.
Fires in the fire place, Couple's Bowling.
Special events at White Eagle Club dining and dancing.
Newtons, Huigens, Rousseaus, and Rices.
Williamses, Wilsons, Powers, and Theisses.
Helping to make Alleluia Church a go.
Watching it miraculously grow.
Taking pride in making our house a home.
Enjoying our empty nest and being alone.
Notes for each other left behind.
Candies you leave for me to find.
Time spent in our swing or hammock on the deck.
You giving me a surprise hug and peck.
Always loving to hear,
Sweet things whispered in my ear.
Thank you for twenty-five years of marriage we celebrate today,
And the memory threads that never fade away.
November 16, 1993

Forty-eight Lines

Handsome husband, married for forty-eight years.
Let's celebrate with forty-eight cheers.
As Bride and Groom, we began our married life,
And vowed to be loving Husband and Wife.

Fort Knox and Army days led to Fort Sill and Pershing missile ways.
And shortly after we were wed, you
shipped out to Vietnam instead.
But God protected you in the palm of His hand.
You returned safely from Vietnam's war-torn land.

Memories of our moving ten times.
Job and life changes were the reason and rhyme.
Daughters born, their growing-up years.
Love, laughter, and of course some tears.

Lifelong friends met along the way,
Making our lives special each day.
Family fun visits and special occasions
Growing up and changing seasons.

Sports, hobbies, music, and recreational fun,
Our tapestry grew as new threads were woven and spun.
Ron's Fireman's Fund and Paul Davis Restoration working days.
Mothering, volunteering, and teaching were Linda's ways.

Our churches, faith, and prayers helped us survive tough times,
When life gave us challenges, dirt, and grime.
Our family was a miracle, for all to see.
More unexpected miracles were meant to be.

Daughters dating brought mates with weddings to follow.
Walking daughters down the aisle, hard to swallow.
Their husbands soon became awesome sons,
And being together was always fun.

Just when you think life cannot get better,
We became Grandparent Club members forever.
Babysitting, sleep overs, days at the pool or park,
Funny things the grandchildren said, made us happy as a lark.

Their sweet hugs, kisses, and beautiful faces,
Kept us visiting and going fun places.
Watching them grow, seeing personalities change.
Each one unique and special in a broad range.

Retirement and moving to Florida sun
Was not easy, but we are having fun.
Our beautiful Villa and wonderful new friends,
Golfing or swimming, good times never end.

Sarasota living, new, fun things to do.
How did life get so full for us two?
Blessings upon blessings along our way,
Making us so grateful every day.

Handsome husband of forty-eight years,
Let's celebrate with forty-eight cheers.
I'm so glad I married the man of my dreams.
Looking forward to you being part of my schemes.
November 16, 2016

Take The Challenge

Happy *forty-ninth* anniversary. We have one year to go,
Until we celebrate our big five oh.
As we think back on our wedding day,
Thought this calendar would be a fun way,
To remember and relive those special parts,
Of two people sharing the love in their hearts!
So as each month comes and goes,
Displayed—a special wedding day pose.

Now here is the challenge to reach our dream,
On the sixteenth of each month, we both must scheme,
To set aside that one day,
To do something that we've wanted to do along the way,
But for some reason never find the time.
No reason or rhyme.
Go to the Selby Gardens and read a book,
Relaxing on the benches, the bay to overlook.

Bike ride through Rothenbach Park,
Sit poolside looking for stars in the dark.
Spend the day together at the pool.
Enjoy the hot tub, have a drink to stay cool.
Listen to the waves, as we take a walk on the beach.
Have a snack—some strawberries and a peach,
Or stay home and swim or float in our pool.
That could be interesting and pretty cool!

Go see Historic Spanish Point off Tamiami Trail.
The outdoor museum looks fun when ads come in the mail.
Or see the show at Big Cat Habitat.

If we sit in the sun, remind me to take a sun hat.
And you may think this a bit strange,
But I will go with you to the shooting range.
Visit Cape Kennedy or Washington, D.C.
Or take a cruise—something different to see.
These are just some ideas that would be fun,
As we celebrate our forty-ninth anniversary in the Sarasota sun.
Happy anniversary. May we have many more!
Looking forward to what life has in store!
November 16, 2017

Forty-nine Years
and Counting

Forty-nine married years and counting, a few months to go,
Until we make it to fifty years, so we can show
Family and friends how it's done,
Fifty Years of Marriage, victory won.

Love will always find a way.
It helped us live each day.
Memories, adventures, highs, and lows,
God helped us navigate life's ebbs and flows.

Now a new challenge lies ahead,
But when all is done and said,
There is no way God can ignore,
All the prayers from shore to shore.

Cleveland Clinic Surgery may seem a fright,
But we will all help you fight, Fight, FIGHT!
Your family, friends, faith, hope will see you through,
Each day in all you will need to do!
Rehab may be a struggle
But you need to get well so we can forever cuddle.
April 21, 2018

Ron was scheduled to have two heart valves replaced until a Sarasota doctor decided surgery was too treacherous for him to attempt. Without surgery, Ron had maybe six months to live. Our only other option, Cleveland Clinic. All medical information had been sent, time was running out for an answer. Would Cleveland Clinic accept Ron? Out of desperation, I phoned the clinic, talked with the head nurse who listened to my plea and placed Ron's medical file on the top of a pile of possible surgeries for Dr. Pettersson, who was just returning from a vacation. Within days, we were on our way to Cleveland. Our daughter set up a Facebook Page where she posted updates. People from coast to coast were praying and sending well wishes. On April 25, 2018, Ron had a successful, ten-hour heart valves-replacement surgery. A chest bleed, the next day, required another surgery. Two pacemaker surgeries would follow for a total of four surgeries at the Cleveland Clinic. Four lung surgeries in Sarasota would occur that fall. Ron worked hard to recover, dealing with diabetes, lung, kidney, and heart challenges. He is a fighter, and God has been faithful during his recovery journey. .

An Invitation to our Celebration

November 16, 2018, Save the date.
Fiftieth Anniversary, come help us celebrate.
Dinner at the Rosemary to dine.
We'll have some good food and wine.
That's a Friday night, six thirty, don't be late.
RSVP to Linda Potter if you can make the date.

What I've Learned Along the Way

❦

Fifty years of marriage, what can I say?
A day to celebrate blessings along the way.
You were that special, softball player, at center field,
By your kisses, your love for me, was sealed.

A handsome athlete in a Jiffy uniform, you stole my heart.
Courageous soldier in war, we prayed would be safe and smart.
A life spent together because of *love*
And watching over us by *God* above.

A family of daughters, their mates, and grandchildren six,
That added love, laughter, learning, and adventures to the mix.
Many caring friends we met along the way
As we moved from place to place to stay.

Friends who became extended family.
Friends there to help whatever the need be.
Louisville, Minnetonka, Los Angeles
Just a few of our home sites along the way.

San Francisco, Indianapolis, Naperville, Illinois,
Now we are retired in Sarasota, golf cart for a toy.
We worked hard, you provided well.
The fruits of your labor paid off, I do tell.

A loving, loyal, advice-sharing Dad to our Jen and Jill.
You're still looking out and coaching, for their best interest and will.
Along came Jason and Tony, each taking a daughter for his wife,
Adding an exciting, interesting, wonderful layer to our life.

The precious jewels in your kingly crown
Are six grandchildren who make you smile, not frown.
Following their sports team success,
And encouraging them in their progress.

The hours you spend talking with and helping friends so dear.
Friends that are far, friends that are near.
Your love of learning new birds in our Heritage Oaks view.
Photographing the incredible colors of the sky and clouds, too.

Your passion for flowers, growing things in the soil.
Gardening skills—to you it is fun and relaxing, not toil.
Career successes, moving with your jobs.
Positive times, but also some sobs.

You ask, *What have I learned along the way?*
Be an angel during the day,
And a devil in bed at night.
Be the first to apologize after a fight.

Slow down, don't move too fast.
Try to make the morning last.
Take time to smell the roses along the way
As long as allergies don't hold you at bay.
Talk with your hubby and listen to what he has to say.

The way to a man's heart is through his tummy.
Make sure your lasagna is not dry, but moist and yummy.

Let your hubby take you to dinner after golfing in the sun so bright
To avoid answering the question, *What's for dinner tonight?*

Honey, you were my Soldier Boy, my Vietnam hero.
Fifty years, we're retired and living in Heritage Oaks.
Fifty fantastic years, wait. This past year has been a little frantic,
But most of those fifty years were fabulous and fantastic.
Fifty years, what else can I say?
We've made it Honey. Let's celebrate today.
November 16, 2018

Kaleidoscope

Love was Blue.
For us, two.
You in Vietnam, so far away.
Me praying for your safety each day.
Sadness and tears,
Hopes and fears!

Love was Yellow.
My returning soldier fellow!
Our future was suddenly sunny and bright.
Prayers answered, we walked in new light.

Love was Green.
Years were lean,
Newness like spring,
Our life together did bring.
Apartment, houses, yards,
Sports and golf games parred.
Church, careers, family fun,
Moving for different climate's sun.

Love was Red.
Our passion fed.
Keeping it alive, you ask how?
Those hugs and kisses—WOW!

Love was Purple.
We tried to follow a good example.
Jennifer and Jill arrived on the scene.
Linda was Ron's royal Queen.

European travels, vacation trips,
Moving to new cities and cruising ships.
He provided well for his family.
They had a wonderful life as good as could be.

Love was Brown.
Life was up and down.
Teen, then college years,
Weddings with bubbles and cheers.
If brown is made from green and red,
New life and passion, what more to be said?

Love was Black.
But Love and hope never lacked.
Infertility, surgeries, jobs end, time mends.
Loved ones lost, feelings tossed.
Life tests, straining the best.

Love was White.
Seeing new light!
Grand-babies born. No more forlorn.
Bodies healing, bring new meaning
To extended family praising.

Love was Orange.
Which is the color for fall.
Grandchildren always bring joy, having a ball.
The baby years of cuddles and hugs,
Childhood days of toys and smiling, cute mugs.
Teen years of sporting events and college choices,
Learning to drive and grandparent voices.

Here's to my husband of fifty-one years,
As we celebrate with friends and cheers.

The colors of our married life,
Of handsome husband and beautiful wife,
Make up a kaleidoscope, a rainbow of love and hope.
How miraculously you have recovered since last year.
Happy fifty-first anniversary to my husband dear.
November 16, 2019

Was It Because. . .

Fifty-one years and still going strong!
Was it because we always got along?

Was it because together we did belong?
Was it because I am the ding and you are the dong?

Was it because you came when I rang the dinner gong?
Was it because one of us was headstrong?

Was it because on Thursdays I played Mah-Jongg?
Was it because we promised to stay together our whole life long?

Was it because we cuddle all night long?
Was it because of a love song?

Was it because of a black sexy thong?
Was it because we made up when we were wrong?

Fifty-one years and still going strong!
Tonight, with friends, enjoying Neil Diamond songs!

We've proven, Love will find a way,
Regardless of what happens each day!
November 16, 2019

Life

You dream
 You plan
  You envision
   You hope
    You love

And one day you realize
 How many of your dreams have come true.
  Your plans have worked out.
   Your visions are realities.
    Your hopes are your reassurances.
     Your love is your bond.

You know it happened because of one special person who
Shared and cared
 Loved and trusted
  Honored and cherished
   Hoped and dreamed
    With you and for you.

You see clearly how deeply that person feels!
 And you count your blessings because of all the goodness.

Anniversary Threads

Create My Tapestry

Poems to celebrate their special day,
For friends we met along the way.
Family members we hope will strive,
To keep that special spark alive.

Friends and Family

Irvin Messel married Phyllis Kanzler at World War II's end.
Fifty-one married, years together they would spend.
Linda and Connie, their daughters, two
Would each get married and say, *I Do.*
Granddaughters Jennifer and Jill
Married Tony and Jason, what a thrill.
Whether family or friends along the way
Just had to have a poem to say,
Congratulations, Happy Anniversary,
Keep love in a marriage, that's the key.

Happy Thirteenth

Happy thirteenth anniversary.
Hope you both are happy as can be.

Hope there's fulfillment in all things you do.
Contentment in your Ankeny life, too.

Enjoyment as your family has fun.
And most days have plenty fresh air and sun.

May there be love in your beautiful house.
Plenty of hugs and kisses for your spouse.

May there be peace between the dog and cats.
No lost books, homework, socks, gloves, boots, or hats.

May the years ahead fulfill all your dreams.
As with excitement, you both plan your schemes.

Happy anniversary today.
May you celebrate in a special way.
Jennifer and Tony, November 23, 2012

Miracle Babies

Twenty years of married life,
Twenty years as husband and wife.
Wedding day bells were ringing,
First-grade class was singing,
Exiting the church, bubbles blown in the air,
Wedding party toured Naperville, trolley ride flair.
River walk photos on that fall day were taken,
Love in the Air, this couple was maken.

Turn of the century, Hawaiian honeymoon.
Palm trees and sun, a romantic time to spoon.
Jobs and each with a career,
Traveling, teaching, hunting deer.
New home, big yard too.
Flower beds and garden to do.
Pets and plants and fabulous decorating,
Kuper Kastle for Queen and King.

Prayers and hopes, ups and downs.
Doctors and meds, smiles and frowns.
Waiting years, doubts and maybes.
Then one day, miracle babies.
Ella first, then Livy Lou.
I can still hear those babies coo.
Their family was complete with those ladies, two.
For husband and wife,
New blessings in their life.

They moved from Plainfield, Illinois
To Ankeny, Iowa, don't forget a single toy.
Family fun, days in the sun.
Ladies growing, Mom and Dad mowing.

Trampoline, cats, and a dog.
Basement window well with a frog.
Quickly the years go past.
Hunting, soccer, will piano lessons last?
Volleyball game or a cross-country run.
Winter snow, Florida spring break fun.

Xylophone and percussion band,
Loading the trailer takes every hand.
Both ladies always have good grades at school.
They study hard and live by the Golden Rule.
Hardworking Mom and Dad,
Friends think the parents are A-OK rad.
Loving family of four,
Always giving so much more.

Bride and groom, husband and wife,
What a compassionate, full life.
Helpful, thankful, hugs and kisses.
Laughing, dreaming, grateful Mr. and Mrs.
Molding their children, being a good friend,
Always lending the time, a listening ear to bend.
Going the extra mile
Giving others an extra smile.

An amazing marriage, is all we can say
They've carved out a life their own special way.
Happy twentieth anniversary. Celebrate your special day,
In your own fun-loving, special way.

May God always keep you in his care
As you continue your love to share.
Much love and lots of hugs and kisses.
And many more happy anniversary wishes.
Jennifer and Tony, November 23, 2019

Tremendous Twenty-two Years

Happy twenty-second anniversary.
For each other, you were meant to be.
Meeting while students at Indiana University.
It didn't take long for both of you to see
A Tri Delta together with a Fiji.
Love, laughter, life together,
Dreams, schemes, together forever.
Engagement plans, atop the Sears Tower,
Timing crucial, before it closed, dire.
Wedding party, handsome groomsmen, beautiful bridesmaids,
Electric sparks as *I do* wedding vows excitedly were said.

Chosen careers, long working, teaching, coaching ways.
Soon there were babies and parenting days.
Family fun, all of us living close by.
Sharing easy ways of getting together to say, *Hi.*
Tanny and Pappy blessed to be
Grandparent Club Members, one, two, three.
Shelby, then Taylor, two precious daughters,
to make it the Storm Crew Four.
Jackson, a fourth of July firecracker son, they would score.
Before babies, a Naperville apartment,
For their family, a Plainfield, Illinois, home was meant.
But their family did not feel complete,
Soon JT was born for the world to meet.
The Storm Crew Six, always a meal to fix.
Toddler-year cute pictures for the mix.

Jill helped start Paul Davis Restoration with Pappy.
Babysitting the grandchildren with Tanny.
From baby bibs, toddler toys, and preschool,
To Bloomington, Indiana, and elementary school.
Running marathons, job choice changes,
School fundraisers, sports team photo pages.
Volunteering, score keeping, meet a friend for lunch,
Yard work, housework, laundry, a bunch.
Jason scrubbing into tons of surgeries,
So many patients would be *good as new* can be.
From middle school, high school to university days.
Six family members times sports teams, homework, no way!

Baseball, Biking, Football, Gymnastics,
Horseback Riding, Basketball,
Running, Skate boarding, Tennis, Track, Volleyball.
When it comes to sports and making that healthy choice,
The Storm Crew works hard staying in shape, we hear their voice.

Life can throw curve balls at any moment.
Your ups and downs, smiles and frowns, well spent.
Loving, supporting, forgiving, redefining, believing,
Encouraging, studying, learning, worshipping, praying.
The Storm Crew Six proved, *love will find a way.*
God will bring strength and healing each day.

Fearlessly finding a way to make life better
Kelly School of Business for Jill, a winner.
Jason helping family by getting his license to sell real estate,
Finding ways to reach patients during the COVID-19 wait.
Sharing their time, helping their friends
Raise the money needed to make amends.
Counseling sessions, encouragement given
When life struggles to the edge have driven.

Taking a friend for cancer treatments,
Believing, hoping, praying for improvements.
Opening the Storm home to their kids' friends,
Treating them with dignity, respect, a listening ear to lend.

On Mother's Day, a four-page letter to Jill was sent.
Listing comments from the friends who spent
Many hours, many days in the loving, caring ways
Of Mama Jill and her special skill,
Of listening, helping, redirecting will.
Boys and girls keep coming back still.
Forgiveness, spiritual guidance, they never get their fill.

Jason and Jill, you have made a tremendous team,
Successfully working, providing, sacrificing, it would seem.
Happy twenty-second anniversary day.
May you celebrate in a special way.
Jill and Jason, June 20, 2020

Tony and Jennifer

From wedding day to wonderful life.

From groom and bride to husband and wife.

From the two of you to a family of four,

And a life of love, laughter and so much more.

Happy seventeenth wedding anniversary

Much love and lots of hugs,

Mom and Dad

Jennifer and Tony, November 23, 2016

Ryan and Lindsey

We read about how the two of you met.
Sounds like it was meant to be!
So many things in common.
The rest was history.

Your engagement was so romantic,
Surprising in such a special way.
Engaged on June third,
That is my birthday.

Your wedding gift's arriving,
By July twelfth, in the mail,
No gift enclosure card,
On my part a fail.

It should be a rectangular piece,
Le Creuset Stoneware
Made for years of serving
Lots of delicious fare.

It may not show up as purchased
On your registry list.
When secured on Amazon Prime,
That step was missed.

Hope the time goes quickly,
Until your wedding day.
And may it be special
In every way.
July 9, 2018

Together

Happy anniversary today,
Suanne and Jere! What can we say?
You split your time between two states.
That seems to satisfy both mates.

Thirty-one years of married bliss,
Guess Jere says yes a lot to the little miss.
Together you golf, bike, and run,
And enjoy your time in the sun.

Dog races, Mah-Jongg, working out.
You two stay busy being out and about.
Updating and decorating your beautiful Villa home,
When you return to Minnesota, we feel so alone.

Dining out for a special meal of fish
Or eating in and sharing a homemade dish.
It is just fun being with you two
Whenever and whatever we do!

Girls day shopping or art and craft fairs,
We definitely have done our share.
As you celebrate thirty-one years, looking back,
For making friends and family memories, you have a knack.

Thirty-one years of blessings to count.
Present-day challenges to mount.
God's faithfulness in the past.
His grace and healing for you both to last.

So here's to our dear roof mates.
Enjoy your special tonight date.
Happy thirty-first anniversary, as the wine your pour.
And may you have many more.
Suanne and Jere, May 2018

Forty Lines for Do Do

Forty years of married life.
Forty years since Roy took Delores for his wife.

Forty years since Roy asked, Will you?
Forty years since Delores replied, I do.

Forty years of babies and bills.
Forty years of struggles up hill.

Forty years of measles and mumps.
Forty years of chicken pox bumps.

Forty years of buying cute dresses.
Forty years of cleaning up messes.

Forty years of laundry and meals.
Forty years of fixing wagon wheels.

Forty years of hopes and dreams.
Forty years of plans and schemes.

Forty years of houses and yards.
Forty years of birthdays and cards.

Forty years of watching seasons come and go.
Forty years of shoveling Minnesota snow.

Forty years of family fun.
Forty years of pleasure for everyone.

Forty years of school, homework, and PTA.
Forty years of carpools and ballgames, hooray.

Forty years of games and bikes.
Forty years of camps and hikes.

Forty years of summer sun.
Forty years of outdoor fun.

Forty years of parenting.
Forty years of babysitting.

Forty years of boys and dates.
Forty years of weddings and mates.

Forty years of nursing and worry.
Forty years of schedules and hurry.

Forty years of prayers sent.
Forty years of support lent.

Forty years, we think that's great.
Forty years married to the same mate.

Forty years of joy and love.
Forty years blessed by God above.

Forty years, what more can we say?
Forty years. Have a special day!
Do Do and Roy, March 14, 1978

I first met Do Do at the Minnetonka Ice Rink, where she provided child care for my daughters so I could have a Mom's Day Out ice skating. Our family had moved to Minnesota from Kentucky, our first move away from family, friends, church, and roots. It was a difficult, cold move, but Do Do came into my life and made it better with her warmth, concern and special care for my children. She will always be a special friend because she gave more than was asked or expected. Her loving generosity touched and changed many lives.

Gator and Dog

July 10, 1976 was the wedding date.
It was true love and passion—not just fate.
Larry, the groom, Dianne, his wife,
Tonight we celebrate forty years of married life.
They raised three, beautiful, unique daughters: Dana, Kelly, Jamie,
Staying busy with school, sports, and special activities.

There were yards to tend and plant, for playing girls.
Hairdos with bangs, straight hair, and curls.
Family fun times, vacations, memories made.
Friends and places etched in their minds, never to fade.
Job transfers, new challenges to face.
Moving meant new friends in a different place.

White Eagle, Naperville was one of those moves.
And it didn't take long to be in their grooves.
Wheatland Elementary and Waubonsie High School.
Golf and volunteering, but soccer would rule.
Downtown Chicago offered weekend fun!
Snow in the winters but summers meant sun.

Homework and Homecomings, friends galore.
Country Club dinners, dances and much more.
It was here in this time of glory
That the Potters and Rices began their story.
But none of us were so bold
To predict what our future together would hold.

Cleveland next, but not for long
As Paul Davis Restoration became their song.
Charleston, South Carolina, Daniel Island, to be exact.
Attempts were made to keep a growing-up family in tact.
Hard working years would definitely pay,
For a motor cycle and boat for play.

Kelly would eventually move to join the pack
As you happily invited her back.
And as I recall she could be seen
In her yellow convertible, looking cool and keen.

Josh would give Jamie an engagement ring.
Then a beautiful outdoor wedding in spring.

They both would work at PDR.
Helping the family business made each a star.
Dana's photography talents certainly made others happy
Including photos taken of the granddaughters of Tanny and Pappy.
Fun with her dogs and lots of introspection,
Living on her own, posting deep reflections!

Their own salon run by the *Daughters Three.*
Hairdos and makeup for weddings are their specialty.
Several warm, inviting homes they built on Daniel Island alone.
Homes beautiful by designing Larry and
decorating Dianne in their zone.
Daniel Island, where golfing is tops!
And for Ron, it became a fun golfing stop.

Gator and Dog have golfed their share,
Won tournaments, trophies, club championships to spare.
Dianne and Linda have always had fun,
Touring, shopping, lunching, beaching in the sun.

And just when you think life can't get any better,
Mason is born, perfect to the letter.

That first grandchild makes you a member,
Of the Grandparent Club forever.
Family has always played a huge part in your lives:
Parents, siblings, nieces, nephews, husbands, and wives!
You both are always there to love and
support friends and family in need
And we are grateful for all you've done for us indeed!

Your energy and interests, artistic talents abound.
And there is always plenty of hospitality to go around.
And now the Cruising Crew Six is back for more fun
To enjoy Caribbean ports and plenty of sun.
So please raise your glasses to celebrate
This fortieth wedding anniversary date!
Dianne and Larry, July 10, 2016

Daughters Four

Happy fiftieth anniversary. What shall we say?
Have a fabulous fiftieth celebration day.
A big celebration is always the time
To remember life's layers, the rhythm and rhyme.
As you look back through those layers of life,
You remember fifty years as husband and wife.

First stop Hawaii and tropical sun.
Navy life, we'll try to make it fun.
Then back to the mainland.
Goodbye surf and sand.
Working jobs and spouses who care.
Your life was special and rare.

Shall we have children, our love to share?
Now four daughters later, each with their own flair.
Life was full of cuddly dolls and pretty dresses,
Hair dos, makeup, and lots of messes.
Then those daughters grew up and did the same.
Marriage, husbands, and babies to name.

St John's Church choir and music to sing.
Wife and husband together they bring
Their special touch to soprano and bass.
Prayer time requests, hands and fingers laced.
Movie Group with popcorn and flick,
Everyone hopes for a good pick.
Discussing the questions, sharing a meal,
Fun Saturday evening, a good deal.

All you do to be involved because you're caring:
Fantasy Football, knitting group, Sunday School sharing.
Sunday brunch or out to dinner,
Our special friendship is a big winner.
And for all those years, what's the reason or rhyme?
Love and Patience got you through each time.
How and why and when and where?
Faith and trust and God and prayer.
Fifty years as husband and wife,
Fifty years to celebrate your Christian life.
Sue and Abe, October 12, 2019

How, Why, When, Where?

Happy fiftieth anniversary. What shall we say?
Have a fabulous fiftieth celebration day.
A big celebration is always the time
To remember life's layers, the rhythm and rhyme.
As you look back through those layers of life,
Fifty years as husband and wife,
How and why and when and where?
Working jobs and spouses who care!

How and why and when and where?
Shall we have children our love to share.
How and why and when and where?
Let's make a different life, something special and rare.
How and why and when and where?
Let's go sailing! Do we dare?
How and why and when and where?
Join a church, volunteer, our fruits to bear.

How and why and when and where?
Initiate Movie Groups for a single or pair.
How and why and when and where?
Fantasy Football league and Men's breakfast Fair.
How and why and when and where?
Sunday School, home visits, Welcome Center, because you care.
How and why and when and where?
Make lemonade when life isn't fair.

How and why and when and where?
Share your home with granddaughter in a snare.
And for the years with no reason or rhyme
Hope, Love, Patience got you through each time.
Fifty years as Husband and Wife,
Fifty years to celebrate your life.
How and why and when and where?
Faith and trust and God and prayer.
Cindy and Alan, September 30, 2019

Hopefully on Time

Dearest friends, Barbara and Jim,
For their fiftieth, an anniversary poem.
So caught up in my rhyme,
Mailed the poem a year early in time.
Barbara being such a jewel,
Never said a word, so I wouldn't feel like a fool.

The following year, June 1, 2018.
Returning home from the Cleveland Clinic scene,
Phoned Barbara, in tears, to say,
Ron had four surgeries in thirty days away.
I have no poem, no card for your special day.

A year too early your poem came to me.
I saved it and am reading it right now, you see.
Barbara's loving grace, dried my tears,
God's provision covered both our memories that year.

That fiftieth anniversary poem cannot be found.
Barbara searched her home, up stairs and down.
In my computer and poetry binder, I took a hard look
Wanting to publish that poem in *My Tapestry of Life* book.

This story just has to be heard.
It is a God thing, not just absurd.
But with so many affected by COVID-19,
Life changes dictated by quarantine.
A missing poem became no big deal.
Importance of life, health, family, friends made real.

Fifty-two years of married life to celebrate,
Fifty-two years of memories you did create,
Louisville, Kentucky home, church, family,
Jiffy Club softball, Stephanie born made three.
We've been friends from the start,
Sharing ideas, hopes, dreams from the heart.

Playing cards, having snacks, so timely.
While our ladies played, then slept so peacefully.
We swapped babysitting for a time to be
Bowling or swimming, to keep our bodies healthy.

Your visits when we moved away,
Visits when we came back, one more hour to stay.
Sharing faith, prayer requests, Bible studies we took.
Each other's insights gave a different perspective look.

The good, the bad, the ugly, the ups and downs.
After phoning to share, smiles instead of frowns.
Miles separated, prevented us from always being there,
Our loving friendship has stood the test of time to bear.

Our husbands, best friends over the years
Church events, travels, aging parent fears.
Job and career changes, softball and sports stories.
Retirement challenges, the good ole days of glory.

Our ladies all grown up, wedding bells, new chapters in life.
Grandchildren, babysitting again, each daughter, a wife.
Our families grew, everyone got older.
Technology proved our grandchildren were smarter.
Their busy lives, so many activities for all.
Hard to stay connected, just give me a call.

And so, as we look through the layers in time
To make sense of the rhythm and rhyme,
Love bound two souls together and always found a way
To nurture hope, trust, faith, peace for life's journey each day.
Joyful blessings from hard work, forgiveness, sacrifice,
The reason Jim's still the husband, Barbara's still his wife.

Happy fifty-second anniversary.
We treasure each fond memory.
Love, health, safety during COVID-19.
May you happily survive the quarantine.
Barbara and Jim, June 1, 2020

Abs, Core, Love

A new fitness director. What would she be like?
We all wondered as we said, good-bye, to Mike.
Jenna was young and trim, fit as can be.
Smart and knowledgeable, we would soon see.

By working our abs, she strengthened our core,
Side planks, front planks, and push-ups galore.
She led classes, attended meetings, offered
group equipment instruction,
Organized road clean-up, blood drives, and
private sessions, one-on-one.

There were warm-up stretches for each and every limb,
Jenna had us wanting to come to classes at the gym.
Three by three by three class was a great workout too.
Stations with balls, weights, and bands that would do.

If you had a hurting muscle or an injury,
Jenna knew the stretch to help, quick as could be.
She even worked with the men in their Prime Time class,
Until they all had achieved a better body mass.

When a yoga instructor was needed, she came through
By getting her certification and started doing Tree Pose, too.
Bosu balance, bridge walks, kayaking adventure,
Goat yoga, meditation relaxation, our ailments to cure.

With her schedule full and over flowing,
She still found time for Paddle Boarding.
Then one day we noticed that sparkle in her eye,
And we all wondered why—was there a guy?

Yes, of course, Jenna had found the *love of her life*.
And then Josh asked her to marry and be his wife.
So, thank you Jenna for all that you do.
We are so happy you are so in *love*, too.

May you have a beautiful Wedding Day and blessings in your life,
As you, Jenna and Josh, become husband and wife.
Joyful wedding wishes. Be happy as can be.
Much love and hugs from your Heritage Oaks family.
Jenna and Josh, September, 2019

Birthday Threads

Create My Tapestry

Husband And Wife

One thread, Ron, my husband
When I, Linda, became his wife.
Many birthday threads we've shared
Throughout our paradise life.

Seventy Years Young

To my wife who is seventy years young.
Many times I feel our life has just begun.
This June, as we celebrate You,
Thought to myself, what would she like to do?

A golf trip, a new driver, a trip in the car?
You need something special, a memory that takes you far.
I can't box a memory or a really good day,
But I can send you somewhere you'll want to stay.

I know how important good friends are to you,
So giving you this ticket is the least I can do.
You can't say No, it's already done.
Time that you went and had some fun.

You leave June thirteenth for five days, a trip just for you,
Hopefully that will give you enough time to pack the right shoe.
Get ready for laughter, lots of talking and sun.
Karen has the week planned and it's going to be fun.

Happy birthday to the *love of my life*.
I am the happiest man to call you my wife.
Linda, June 3, 2017

For my seventieth birthday, my husband surprised me with a plane ticket to Cape Cod to visit my friend Karen for five days. A second surprise, I was joined by both daughters and two other dear friends. My daughter Jennifer helped her father by supplying this poem.

Seventy Surprise

Linda's surprise party's over, returned home and unpacked.
But *love* and *laughter*, when we're together, will never lack.
Thank you for all you did to make a plan come true.
Thank you for friendship, love, and special gifts, too.

The memories of that awesome airport, arrival, surprise,
Forever in my heart and mind, an image that never dies.
Rental car trip to Cape Cod with a stop at the liquor store.
That first image of the ocean and fishing boats on shore.

The poster of Linda with ratted hair beehive.
Balloons flying in the breeze for the arriving five.
Appetizers and lunch and that decadent chocolate cake,
Birthday decorations, Karen's beautiful home, too much to take.

Walking the beach, watching boats unload their fish,
Fresh cod sandwiches, a delicious *melt in your mouth dish*,
Shopping fun at the Cape Home Decor,
Laughing at the cute and funny Ducks Galore.

Father's Day shopping and the *Happy Pappy* T-shirt find.
That will definitely make Ron feel like one of a kind.
Bike rides and workouts that made some feel sore.
Delicious lunches and dinners that made us want more.

Movies each night brought laughter and tears,
As we shared memories of events from other years.
Relaxing in the backyard, catching some sun rays.
Sharing our lives, making the most of our days.

A deep-tissue massage for a special spa day,
Made me feel so relaxed in every way.
In matching sweat shirts, picture taking on steps and in the sand,
Jumping up, trying not to hurt ourselves as we land.

The young and cute parking attendant was so helpful that night,
Taking our group photos, with all his might.
And who could forget our last night drinks.
Add dancing, warm baked cookies, dinner in a wink.
Moscow Mules or Rum Chata with Fireball Whiskey,
Linda missed the movie, hope Saturday, sober she'll be.

Jen, for helping Father come up with a plan.
Jill, for driving the rental as the lead car man.
Dianne and Linda, for taking off work to be part
Of a great surprise that will linger in my heart.
Karen, for so willingly being the best Cape Cod hostess.
Your comfortably decorated home is the ultimate *mostest*.

Thank you for the hours and money you spent.
So very, very much to me it meant,
To celebrate with the cream of the crop.
No better friends could you ever top.
June, 2017

Card Shower Surprise

Dear Friends both Silver and Gold,

Get ready for the saga that's about to unfold.

In Nineteen hundred, forty-five,

Guess who was born, bouncing and alive?

If you can subtract, you've figured it out

Without even taking your calculator out.

June seven is the day, 1985 is the year

That *Ron's big four oh* is finally here.

Wish I could throw a party or even a feast

So we could all celebrate together at least.

But since we're separated by so many miles,

We'll have to forgo the party, do without your smiles.

So I'm asking you for the next best thing.

Please send a card or let the telephone ring.

Let's help Ron celebrate his *big four oh*

By receiving greetings from everyone he knows.

Ron, June 7, 1985

This poem invite was sent to my Christmas Card list of friends who could not join and help us celebrate Ron's fortieth. Friday night I had a small dinner party and read all the cards. For Saturday, I planned for Ron and I to play in a tennis event. Upon arriving home, neighbors and friends had gathered for a surprise party. Ron was totally shocked. A birthday bunny dressed in red and candles that could not be blown out, rounded out the party.

Bring Your Best Story

It's a Surprise Party, to celebrate Ron being fifty.

So please, friends come, that will be nifty.

But bring *no gift. Please no card.*

You may write a poem if you're a bard,

Or share your best story so you can roast,

Or something to say so you can toast

Ron turning the *big five-oh.*

Help his wife and daughters let everyone know.

June 3, 1995 is the day.

Potter's deck, 4018 Broadmoor Circle is the way.

Please arrive at six in the evening. Don't be late.

The Potter family will take Ron to the White Eagle club as bait.

Park on Paradise Canyon so your car won't be seen

Because old Ron is pretty keen.

When Ron returns home, grilled chicken for all.

So bring your best story, help Ron have a ball.

Roast and Toast

Who is this guy we so eagerly roast?
Who is this person we gladly toast?
Born on June 7, 1945,
A seven-pound, eight-ounce boy, bouncing and alive,
Martha and Walter Potter's first born son,
But they had only just begun.
Donnie, Dennis, and Patty, too.
A family of six would nicely do.
Farming and softball on the *Potter Plantation*.
Hunting, fishing, plenty of family fun.
Fern Creek High, cross country, basketball.
Ron was quite the athlete at six feet, three inches tall.
Political Science, baseball trips at U of L,
Until the Army and Uncle Sam rang his bell.
First Fort Knox, then Fort Sill.
His life would have been very nil.

That summer blind date,
Turned into a lifelong mate.
On November 11, 1968, the groom and bride,
Walked down the aisle with wedded pride.
Twenty-eight days later, Vietnam became Ron's test.
For six months, no one had much rest.
Prayers were answered, you returned unharmed.
And each other's hearts were continually warmed.
A job to perform, bills to pay.
Excitement as we moved away.
Twenty-seven years working at Fireman's Fund Insurance Company.
Louisville, Minnetonka, San Francisco to see.

Indianapolis, Los Angeles, Naperville, too.
Great friends in those places we knew.

Sports always played an important part,
Helping you keep a healthy heart.
Softball with Jiffy Club traveling team.
Basketball and tennis, you were lean and mean.
Running became your passion with the Mini Marathon.
You could be seen running at dusk and dawn.
Golfing trips, a *hole in one*,
At White Eagle Course in the May sun.
Yards where we lived, you planted many trees.
That's why you were nicknamed *Ronnie Appleseed*.
Flowers and vegetables you love to plant and watch grow.
You even enjoy blowing away the snow.

But the true joy and pride of your life
Are the daughters born to you and your wife.
Gentle Jennifer with favorite Pooh Bear,
Her sweet smile and golden hair.
Tender, caring heart is Jill Marie,
Hair rubbing her ear, special blanket, *Bunkie*.
Those wonderful growing-up years,
Filled with their laughter, as well as *boy* tears.
Do you realize over half your life,
Spent with this person you call your wife.
Love notes that say, *I love you a bunch*,
Tenderly tucked in my lunch.
Flowers you pick, cards you send,
The night we renewed wedding vows again.

Who is this guy we so eagerly roast?
Who is this person we gladly toast?
Fried chicken is still his number one dish.
Surrounded by loved ones his number one wish.

Fifty years, some say the beginning of a fresh start
For a man with a new heart.
The grilled chicken was my roast.
A gathering of special friends my toast.
Happy fiftieth birthday, Honey. May you have more
Years of wonderful surprises in store.
Ron, June 7, 1995

My Amazing Man

Seventy years and going strong.
Happy Birthday, dear Pappy, as we sing the song.
Seventy years, You are an amazing man.
Seventy years, Always an awesome tan.

Seventy years, With an active childhood on the Potter farmstead.
Seventy years, So many growing up memories in your heart and head.
Seventy years, High school, college, sports teams.
Seventy years, Wasn't it just yesterday? It does seem.

Seventy years, First job with Fireman's Fund, then Army life.
Seventy years, Proud Vietnam Vet and marriage to your beautiful wife.
Seventy years, Working, career, moving place to place.
Seventy years, At times life must have seemed like a race.

Seventy years, Then Jennifer Renee, Jill Marie, and fatherhood memories.
Seventy years, You often wished time would slow down and freeze.
Seventy years, Weddings brought the sons we never had, Jason and Tony.
Seventy years, And life kept getting better for you and me.

Seventy years, Even though there were trials along the way.
Seventy years, The best was yet to come, for on that day,
Seventy years, A Grandfather you became.
Seventy years, And Pappy, became your new name.

Seventy years, Shelby, Taylor, Jackson made three.
Seventh years, Ella, Olivia, and lastly JT.
Seventh years, So many photos and grandparent fun.
Seventh years, Memories of trips to play in the sun.

Seventh years, You've always taken time to plant and smell the roses.
Seventh years, Taken advantage of special places with photo poses.
Seventh years, Calling a friend or lending a hand.
Seventy years, You've always been a helpful man.

Seventy years, You are definitely a man who has left a mark.
Seventy years, Now you are retired and live between Bee Ridge and Clark.
Seventy years, Plenty of time for golfing in your birthday golf cart.
Seventy years, As from one golf hole to another you dart.

Seventy years, Life is good and you will see.
Seventy years, Just how exciting the rest will be!
Seventy years, God has held, protected you in the palm of his hand.
Seventy years, He will continue to help you be his Amazing Man.

Happy seventieth birthday to my honey of a husband
Ron, June 7, 2015

Here's to Seventy-two

I love how you make dinner plans.
In the movie theater or when we walk, you hold my hand.

You are the man of my many dreams.
You help carry out my plans and schemes.

You surprise me with beautiful flowers and sweets,
That bring wonderful fragrances and delicious eats.

You cuddle and snuggle to make me feel loved and safe.
When we eat out, you make it feel like a date.

There are so many things I admire about you.
Hope you know how much I love you, too.

Here's to being seventy-two.
Life still holds much for us to do.

Hope your days are special and fun,
And you have birdies golfing in the sun.

May you have many more birthdays to celebrate,
And wonderful adventure memories with your mate.
Happy birthday
Ron, June 7, 2017

Determination

The blessings of birthdays over seventy-three years,
Celebrating with candles and cheers.

Each year with its own special memories.
Each year comes and goes with ease.

Such a full and meaningful life
Supported by love from friends,
Family, and beautiful wife.

But now we cannot ignore,
We've aged and we both snore.

It may take us longer to get up and down,
Which may change a smile or two into a frown.

This past year was one of medical challenges to face,
That took up most of your time and space.

While we would not have chosen a Cleveland Clinic stay
And being gone most of April and May,

Unfortunately life has given you plenty of lemons,
But as they say
You can make a ton of lemonade today.
Four surgeries and a long hospital stay
Has put you in a state of dismay.

Family and friends know beyond a shadow of a doubt
In due time you will be up and about.

We know your desires, determination, and drive
Will make you work hard to rehab and stay healthily alive!

We are all here cheering for you.
Willing to help in all you need to do.
Happy seventy-third birthday is our wish for you.
And may those new heart valves last a long time, too.
Ron, June 7, 2018

Pappy

Mom: We call you *Pappy*.
You are awesome, generous, and snappy.

Jen: Your love for family is so great.
It shines through your actions and ideas for family and mate.
You are the *rock* to which we always turn.
For suggestions, ideas, answers, and advice, we always yearn.

Jason: You cut the grass on the riding lawn mower.
Got the yard mulched, what a chore.
Planted flowers, hung a flowering basket.
Had dead bushes removed, now the yard is fit.

Jill: You tried celery juice and sleeping with the cat.
And when someone needs help, you go to bat.
Taking me to work, out to lunch,
We all love you a great big bunch.

Olivia and JT:
You don't like losing to us at *Big two* card game.
But we love playing and winning just like you, just the same.

JT: You've encouraged us to stay with our sports,
Even when we were out of sorts.

Olivia: You've enjoyed our music and art,
And always make us feel extra smart.

Jackson: You've taken me to football practice most every day
And stopped for food along the way.

Met my new friends and supported my choice
To transfer to South High School, understanding my voice.

Ella: We love your pride when we win or make good grades,
And encourage us when we lose and the glory fades.
You've followed our daily activities
And stay in touch which makes us feel pleased.
My hunting score and volleyball game,
You just want to know I'm happy and sane.

Taylor: Cheering me on at volleyball and track meets,
Supporting me when I thought I was beat.
Sharing sectionals and Indiana High School State,
Breaking school records, sixth place on the podium. That was great.

Shelby: High school graduation activities, you were a part.
You've been there for each grade from the start.
My photo shoot at Sample Gates, Indiana University campus, IU.
Watched me get my diploma at Graduation Ceremony, too.
So many memories from eighteen years past
Will always be cherished in my heart to last.

All: So today we want to *celebrate* your life, *Pappy*.
And we want you to *just be happy*.
Happy seventy-fourth Birthday.
Pappy, June 7, 2019

Seventy-five

Days come, days go
Do we ever really know
What our life will have in store?
Will there be less, will there be more?
Birthdays are a special time
To reflect on reason and rhyme.

Seventy-five years and still very alive.
Going strong, proving nay sayers wrong.
Hours and months of *muscle reactivation.*
Exercises, weights, squats, tread mill fun?

Shelby's graduation party for high school years.
Pappy's photos, friends, memories, decorations, food, cheers.
Before her Freshman year began, after her summer internship,
To Sarasota, she made a quick trip.
Rain, Siesta Beach fun, rain, fish dinner at Philippi Creek,
Funny face photos, Abel's ice cream treat.

Minnesota, Vermilion Lake trip for golf and fishing,
Ice cream in the morning, double-dipping,
Log house, eating their catch of fish, Ron and Harry
Relaxing by the lake with Jack and Kerry.

Larry and Dianne Rice, Rick and Linda Gunder visit.
St. Armands shops, lunch, pool, lift our spirits.
The *cruising six* enjoyed your delicious salmon on the grill.
Strawberry pie and marinade magic, made dinner a thrill.

Our villa was painted, spectacular night sky sunsets,
Deer, Heron, Sandhill Cranes, Roseate Spoonbill, Egrets.
Fall road trip, drove four thousand miles
To experience grandchildren's sports, hugs, and smiles.

Bloomington, Indiana, and the Storm Crew,
Jackson and JT's football games, Shelby's dorm room, too.
Taylor's volleyball games, canning pickles,
Brown County candles, Louisville trip to see the Driskells.
Helped Jason with garage and yard, lunches with Jill,
Keeping up with practices, you are not over the hill!

Ankeny, Iowa, Kuper Crew next stop.
Livy playing xylophone at football halftime, over the top.
Watching Ella score at volleyball, such fun
Her homecoming dance prep, makeup, hairdo, photo run.
Roasted and toasted Tony's fiftieth birthday,
Kupers' twentieth anniversary, Happy sweet sixteen, Ella, we say.

Dined with friends, O'Neils and Emerys to celebrate
Fifty years of marriage to their mate.
We celebrated our fifty-first anniversary,
Neil Diamond Impersonator Dinner Concert to see.

Pensacola trip with friends to see the plane Navy Pilot Harry flew,
Naval Air Station, Blue Angels, museum, training academy, too.
Walking the beach, playing card games, dinners out.
Fitness time, movie night, good people it's all about.

Remember helping make cookies for Storms at Christmas-time?
They enjoyed Big Cat Habitat, gifts with Tanny's rhymes.
Shopping, tennis, hot tub, golf cart rides, golfing.
Working out to stay fit, then Christmas-time eating.

Pat and Steve visit, January Sarasota sun.
Pat and Linda witness dinner and Menopause fun.
Greater Vision Gospel Hymn Concert in Tampa
Inspirational voices and singing with the piano.

Trip to New Orleans, oysters on the half shell, shrimp and grits.
Half-day bus tour, historic city pieces and bits.
National World War II Museum two days spent
Listening to audio accounts of heroes sent
Into Hitler or Japanese harm's way.
Old films showing battles, bombings each day.

Venues where bombs caused your seat to rock,
Snow falling on the audience as on movie screen mock.
Warehouse entire wall of world's countries affected.
Salvation would come when the U.S., to enter the war, elected.
The rolling movie showed the entire war from beginning to end.
Thankfully Good won over Evil. The world could begin to mend.

Spring Break, Jill and JT arrive for Florida sun.
Taylor and Shelby in Florida with friends for fun.
Jackson home with Jason for basketball.
JT had tennis lessons, golf with Pappy, then we hit the virus wall.
Jill worked from Florida, Pappy finally won at Big Two.
The Storms returned home for Taylor's eighteenth birthday do.

Thankfully everyone is doing well
We've been indoors for quite a spell.
As sun bathes our Florida Room
The orchids are in gorgeous bloom.
Ron's watering and fertilizing,
Healthy growth to green plants and flowers bring.

The purpose of this poem, to show you, dear,
Once again you've had an incredible year.
The pandemic coronavirus has made it clear,
Whatever life brings our way, we can survive each day.
Happy seventy-fifth birthday.
Ron, June 7, 2020

Birthday Threads

Create my Tapestry

Daughters

Threads for my Daughters Dear,
The wind beneath my wings,
Always near to help and steer.
Jennifer and Jill make my heart sing.

Sons-by-Marriage

Threads added for sons I never birthed.
Now bring love, laughter, and mirth.
Tony and Jason created amazing families.
Hard working pillars they will always be.

Healing Humor

Your Cleveland Clinic Column kept all in the know.
The photos you posted were quite the show.
Your humorous updates and timely wit,
With your reading audience, you were always a hit.
You faithfully nursed your father dear.
Always at bedside, always near.
Spending the night or helping him groom,
Supplying and organizing the snacks in his room.

Dealing with nursing staff and other assistants,
Helping him walk, witnessing the scrotum dance.
You secured dinners, uber drivers, and booked air flights.
Rode in a police car, to the Clinic, in the middle of the night.
We laughed at George McArdle's attack,
Jesus took one look at Ron, and sent him back.
You had encouraging words when there were tears,
And knew Pappy would live for many more years.

Daughter, wife, mother, friend,
Teacher, sister—the list has no end.
Fun aunt to nephews and nieces.
Life coach when lives are in pieces.
Now we can add nurse and caregiver to the list.
If Cleveland Clinic hadn't happened, special bonding we'd missed.
And so on your birthday we just want to say,
Thank goodness Pappy is home from his hospital stay.

Thank you for all the love, support, and beauty you bring
To our family, summer, fall, winter, and spring.

Your gentle, healing, loving ways,
Your smile and humor that lingers and stays
In our hearts and thoughts always.
Hope this is one of your best birthdays.
All our love and lots of hugs and kisses.
And tons of happy forty-sixth birthday wishes.
Jennifer, June 23, 2018

From Childhood to Twenty-one

Jennifer, go to sleep. Angels watch and angels keep over you until the sun shines through. Mom and Daddy love you too. Hug your Pooh, hug your Pooh, hug your Pooh the whole night through, until morning sunshine wakes you two. Now go to sleep, my Love.

Living in Louisville, we lullabied you to sleep each night,
Your Winnie the Pooh bear watching over 'till morning light.
You loved to rub his nose and Paw Paw's, too.
Will you ever outgrow that? I haven't a clue.

Everything you did was a wonderful first for you...
First words, first step, first tooth, charmed us too.
Your baby body tanned from Hi Li sun.
You'd hold on tight for bike ride fun.

You helped us name and watch over baby sister Jill.
It's heartwarming to see you remain best friends still.
You recited the Christmas Story and lots of rhymes,
Watched Mr. Rogers's TV program many times.
Loved blocks, puzzles, your Shape-O toy.
Library story hour, with puppets, for you was a joy.

Started school in Minneapolis and rode your first bus.
Learned to count and read, which amazed us.
Floated on your back in Minnetonka, Lake Ann.
At the neighborhood pond, fed ducks from your hand.

In Indianapolis, you enjoyed dance class,
Girl Scouts, Children's Choir,
Cello, piano, and for swimming had quite a desire.

You've moved from Louisville to Minnetonka to San Ramon,
Indianapolis to Newbury Park and now Naperville is home.

Hairdos, makeup, nail polish fuss,
Your girl and boy friends were also fun for us.
Fancy dresses, parties, your first high heels.
Homecomings, proms, and dates with their own wheels.

High school memories and college success,
Dreams for a career in teaching and counseling, no less.
Loving, caring, sweet as can be.
Kept for a special purpose, can't you see?

Seems like yesterday I phoned the ball park and said,
Send home Ron Potter. This is Code Red!
Send home Ron Potter, I don't mean to home plate.
His wife needs to get to the hospital and can't be late!

That next morning with Daddy by my side,
Miss Jennifer was born. Five days later taking her first auto ride.
And now you're driving, thriving, a Delta Zeta college gal,
A working woman with a certain young man your best pal.

The years have gone quickly as I look back today.
But the memories I'll cherish in my heart to stay.
Baptized, confirmed, each day we prayed over you.
Our prayers for today: *God will always watch over you, too.*

As we celebrate with birthday fun,
We realize your childhood's done.
It's hard to believe you are already twenty-one.
Yes, all grown up and twenty-one.
Jennifer, June 23, 1993

May You Find

On this your forty-seventh birthday

J oy in all you choose to fill your day.

E nergy abundant to use along your way.

IN ner peace through your faith and rest.

N othing hindering your happiness.

I n a sunrise and sunset, beauty find.

F amily and friends be loving and kind.

E njoyment of a very good book.

R elaxation and renewal in your favorite nook.

Jennifer, June 23, 2019

Joyful for Jennifer

I cannot believe my baby daughter is
celebrating her forty-eighth birthday.
So many beautiful blessings, magical
memories, family fun along the way.
To be complete, your parents wanted a family.
After three years, the hope, the dream, reality.

Growing years, Father's career relocations,
Neighborhood friends, scenic sensations,
Classroom projects, college and sorority events,
Proms, graduations, teaching career, your bent.

Both of us teaching first grade at White Eagle Elementary.
We made newspaper headlines, you and me.
What a tremendous team we shared,
With Mindy, Teresa, Kristy, and Amy we were paired.
To the moon and back we would travel, air packs and space suits.
Marriage vows, your class singing at the wedding, to boot.

Now Tony, Jen, Ella, Olivia, your family of four.
Career changes, moving rearranges, life's tour.
Artistic, creative, domestic, decorating,
Appreciation and love of flowers and gardening.
Masterfully mothering and nurturing those miracle babies.
Happily helping train and nourish them into beautiful ladies.
Active, bright, creative, fun, healthy, intelligent, kind,
Just a few of the attributes on your wall sign.
Like mother, like daughter, that is true.
Your supportive spirit and kind heart we see in them too.

We love the stories you share of your care giving work each day
Clearly see your patience and enjoyment, your gift, your way.
Those you serve have become your friends.
For some, you were there until the final end.
We sense your deep satisfaction and joy each day.
Beautiful blessings, magical memories, family fun along the way.
Happy forty-eighth birthday.
Jennifer, June 23, 2020

Daughter, Friend,
Mother, Wife

Miss Jill Marie, you turn forty on Saturday.
We hope you have a fabulous birthday.
You've brought so much into everyone's life
By being a *daughter, friend, mother, wife.*

You're the wind beneath our wings on any given day.
I love the way we talk, plan, and pray.
You're the *never back down* person in our family life.
Always there to help in times of stress and strife.

Social justice and helping others is your God-given passion.
Your life shows that with your Cuban Mission.
Loving, supporting, helping your friends,
A daily occurrence that never ends.

As a mother, you are the best.
You function with high energy and little rest.
Advising, teaching, shopping at the mall,
Hairdos, ball teams, practices—you do it all.

Chauffeur, nurse, coach who cares,
Number one cheerleader, always the *mother bear.*
Short-order cook at home, at work, taking a call
Filling orders, business demands, you are on the ball.

When it comes to Jason, a super wife.
Caring, forgiving, the love of his life.
Fun vacations or active family schedules to balance.
Together you've figured out every life challenge.

Eighth-grader, Shelby's cheerleading,
gymnastics, track meets to see,
Intense scholastic homework, teen challenges there will be.
Seventh-grader, Taylor has softball, horse
camp travels, volleyball games,
Hard books to read, and back surgery recovery pains.

Fifth-grader, Jackson's baseball and football,
turning him into a young man.
He likes golfing, friends, shopping the latest trends when he can.
Third-grader, JT, is the quarterback,
running back, having football fun,
Baseball, basketball, golfing, energy never done.

You are a child of God, heaven-sent.
Making a difference is your bent.
Supporting, encouraging, working hard each day.
The Bible, Christian music, and book authors to guide your way.

Daughter, friend, mother, wife.
You bring so many blessings into each life.
So as we celebrate your special *fortieth* birthday,
May this coming year be extra special in every way.
Jill, October 11, 2014

Sweet Memories

Birthdays are times to think about the past
And fun memories that always last.
Spring Break family fun,
Mostly at Lido beach in the sun.

JT digging to China in the sand,
With a shovel and with his hand.
Hot tub, golf cart, eating out,
Black Dog attire and walking about.

The pools, floats, pictures, and poses.
Don't get sunburned noses.
Fun in Orlando, more pools and sun.
Plenty of Taylor's volleyball fun.

Good eats at the Ugly Grouper.
Trying to land a Heartland client, super!
For JT's birthday, another round of TreeUmph
To complete your vacation triumph.

Attending Mom's seventieth birthday surprise,
Chatham, Cape Cod fun, she would never surmise.
Moscow Mules and movies at night,
Delicious meals and chocolate cake delight.
Morning walks and Boutique shopping,
Karen kept us all hopping.

Our August/September visit and stay
Had new challenges each day.
Success at school for all the crew!
Touch down and kicking victories for JT, too.

Taylor's Volleyball wins and newspaper reviews,
Beating South High School was very sweet, too.
Jackson's successful football plays
Have made, for him, a good name in many ways.
Shelby's cheerleading is always a delight to see.
The first victory in two years, this football game, would be.

Selling mums at the football games.
All the new orders and new names.
A garage full of mum flowers!
Too many fund raising hours.

A new family dog, Roscoe, came into your life.
Heartland became your new job as wife.
Keeping score at volleyball games,
Running with the kids and new boyfriend names.

You are not just the bottom line.
You are what helps your family tick and rhyme.
You are an amazing friend,
Supporting and helping the Cross family to the end.

Your compassion and good will,
Have always been and are there still!
You are a blessing to all and to me.
You are exactly what God has called you to be.

Birthdays are times to think of the future,
And wish you the best of everything for sure.
Happy forty-third birthday.

Jill, October 11, 2017

Be Happy

Happy forty-second birthday, Miss Jill Marie.
Hope you're happy as can be.

You are a gracious person with a good heart.
Helping others, because you want to be part
Of the solution, not because you need to,
But because that is what you do.

Have a good workout or run with Roscoe
Before your day starts and you're on the go.
Before school, a fun time with the *fabulous four.*
Hope your day's not a revolving door.

Maybe lunch with a special friend,
Each other's ear to bend.
Time for that special book to read.
Time to reflect on your blessings indeed!

Time through a magazine to look.
A dinner with your hubby, you don't have to cook.
Relax, watch a movie, whatever makes you happy.
Have a great birthday, Love, Tanny and Pappy.
Jill, October 11, 2016

Combo Wishes

Storm Family equals a busy life.
Extra challenges for husband and wife.
Taking care of your children four
Is no simple, easy chore.

You may hear friends talk of only one child,
Life with four teenagers is always exciting and wild.
While your work and sacrifices are times four,
And you may not know who is coming through your open door,
In the end, the rewards are great,
Even when they arrive home late.

The love you give will be returned to you
In pride and joy watching the things they do.
So even though you are both a year older,
Know you both are wiser and bolder.

May the joys of the journey ahead of you,
Outweigh the trials and tribulations, too.
Remember the butterfly can only soar
Because of the struggle out of the cocoon, to bore.

So on your special birthdays,
May you feel blessed in many ways!
May you find joy in the things you do,
And lots of love between you two.

Instead of birthday tickles,
Enjoy your twenty-seven pints of Lime pickles.
Instead of a trip to the moon,
Enjoy your clean garage, closet, and room.

Know we love and miss you,
And think of you often each day too.
Happy forty-fifth, Jill and forty-seventh, Jason.
Jill, October 11, 2019 Jason, October 8, 2019

During a two-week visit, Lime pickles were made and lots of cleaning
and organizing took place. That's what grandparents do.

Forty, Someone Said

Forty I read.
Forty That can't be.
Jason doesn't look that to me.
But then—
Forty is not old if you're a tree.
Forty is the age I used to be.

Forty Love, a tennis score.
You win with one point more.
Forty an OK score for a golf game,
As long as you don't shoot the back nine holes the same.

Forty exercises at the gym and track.
Forty stretches are best for the back.
Forty baskets for a basketball score.
Forty laps around the track, what a chore.

Forty notes, a wide range to sing.
Forty and sporty, has a nice ring.
Forty winks, a short nap.
Forty hugs and kisses from children on your lap.

Forty-plus working hours a week.
Forty phone calls to return in a streak.
Forty chords on a guitar he strums.
Forty tunes Jason gladly hums.

Forty football passes in the front yard.
But coaching those to touchdowns is still hard.
Forty dollars pays a bill.
Forty mph on a hill.

Forty a number found in the Bible several times.
Forty is the amount of four silver dimes.
Forty minutes is a nice walk in the sun.
Forty minutes and the steaks are too done.

Forty almost every state.
Not yet forty, the age of Jason's mate.
Forty the age at which life begins, some say.
He's forty on this Columbus Day.

Forty sounds good to me.
Forty just the age I used to be.
Forty That's actually pretty nifty.
Cause forty sounds better than fifty!
                    Jason, October 8, 2012

You're Forty-four

Jason, Jason Storm,

Birthday wishes are coming your way.
Hope you have an incredible day!

Special time spent with your family,
Probably a sporting activity.

A movie/dinner date with your wife
For a fun memory in your life.

Golf outing with fraternity brothers.
Visiting with your Father and Mother.

Whatever the rhyme or the reason,
So many blessings for your season.

Missing you and wishing we could be there
To help make your birthday without a care.

Jason, October 8, 2016

Forty-five, So Alive

Rising early each morning, for boot camp workout,
Helps Jason stay healthy and trim, no doubt.
Working hard for family.
Always there whatever the need be.

On the road, driving to work at D.J.O.
On the road, rain, sun, or snow.
Kids to school or practice field at night.
Practicing with the kids until they get it right.

Coaching football, helping players make that team connection.
Coaching football, to make that winning touch down run.
Time that could be just for him.
Instead, passing a football or shooting basketballs to the rim.

Witnessing sports successes and victories,
Volleyball, cheerleading, football, he always sees.
Husband, Father, Friend, and Son,
He makes time for family and fun.

Taking his family to church on Sunday,
To feed the soul, meditate, and pray.
He can be seen riding his John Deere,
His huge yard professionally perfect, darn near.

Cleaning, organizing, moving mums,
Trash Days with stickers—he may need a Tums.
Homework, sports, jobs, and more.
Careful scheduling is quite the chore.

Six busy people whose lives are never a bore,
Sometimes the house seems like a revolving door.
But when push comes to shove and a friend is in need,
Jason is one hundred percent there indeed.

Calls to doctors, hospital visits, hours of talking.
Organizing *Go, Fund, Me*, the extra miles he is walking.
Sweet-talking the Bloomington auto dealer,
A car for the Cross family for $1.00, what a *stealer*.

The Cross family is blessed to be
Such good friends with the Storm family.
We celebrate your forty-five years of life!
Regardless of the trials and strife.

We are honored to see the choices you make.
Hope you enjoy your ice cream and cake.
Happy forty-fifth birthday.
Jason, October 8, 2017

$$$$ Is Honey

Candy is dandy,
But I say, $$$$ is honey.
It will buy a sweet treat,
Or a meal of veggies and meat.

It will buy clothes for your bod,
Or fish for the grill, salmon or cod.
It will buy a movie with yummy snacks,
Or save it and stay at home and relax.

It will buy gas for your car,
Or a game of golf, let's hope for a par.
It will buy hunting or fishing gear,
Or auto repair so car is easier to steer.

It will buy services to enjoy,
Or new equipment or new toy.
It will buy tickets for a sporting event,
Or fix the fender if it is bent.

It will buy tennis shoes or maybe just the laces,
Or given to the dentist for teeth braces.
However you decide to spend it,
Hope it is the perfect fit.
Happy birthday

Behind the Garage Door

🏵

Fifty, I heard someone say.
Fifty years on his next birthday.
Fifty is not old if you're a tree.
Fifty, the age I used to be.

Fifty, thought it would be fun to explore,
Fifty, all the stuff on the other side of the garage door.

Fifty-plus duck decoys of all sizes and shapes,
Fifty-plus bottles of glue, and bungee cords and duct tape.
Numerous mounted heads of deer and bear.
Fifty turkey feathers, antlers, nuts, bolts, give his garage flair.

Fifty-plus pieces of barn and tree wood, short or tall,
Crafted into decorative shelves for window and wall.
Or a desk for study and homework.
Dad is so handy—what a perk!

Fifty-plus storage bins, fishing poles, tubes, electrical cords,
Stuff he may need in future time, he likes to hoard.
Fifty-plus bags in his hunting freezers:
Venison, duck, unknown items with feathers and fur.

Fifty-plus ball-type hats and all sorts of tools.
Camouflage hunting and fishing gear to stay dry, warm, or cool.
Fifty-plus lanterns and brooms, and all kinds of sprays
Needed for bees or wasps on any day.

Fifty-plus hours of hunting and fishing during season.
Time spent with Ella, Olivia, Jen, and good friends, the reason.

Fifty-plus additions turned the yard into a peaceful atmosphere.
Beautifully potted flowers and yard art his wife holds dear.

Driftwood, grasses, flower beds, and trees,
Dinner bell and bird feeders to watch the birds feed.
Fifty-plus bricks laid to make the patio,
Fire pit, outdoor furniture, and gazebo.

Fifty-plus spices, rubs, and marinades for outdoor grilling
Tasty delicious meals for eating and enjoying.

Fifty-plus hours working hard each week,
Illinois, Iowa, Nebraska for AWIP, his sales to peak.

Fifty ways he knows to make things better,
Sewing on a button or mending a sweater.
Fifty years of always helping a friend
Or finding a way to make it mend.

Tony, we've seen your core values in action.
Your love, patience, forgiveness, and having fun,
Kindness, fairness, respect, and creativity
Is seen in all you do and want to be.

May you have an enjoyable, fiftieth birthday.
And celebrate in your own way.
Tony, November 5, 2019

Birthday Threads

Create my Tapestry

Grandchildren

Many threads for my grandchildren six.
New love, hope, and dreams added to the mix.
Membership to the Grandparents' Club.
Now my life is a busier hub.
Storm Crew: Shelby, Taylor, Jackson, JT.
Kuper Crew: Ella, Olivia. Unique lives meant to be.

Countdown

Let the countdown begin.
Admitted to Indiana University. That's a big win.

Classes connecting you to Kelly Career Center,
In case your accounting class leads to a business venture.

Sociology—social problems understood with your unique mind.
Philosophy will help you search for wisdom to find.

Challenging classes, but you are so smart.
Studying and succeeding are to you an art.

A roommate you adore.
Just like you—organization is not a chore.

Seventh-floor dorm room in Briscoe with a great view.
Fixed up with twinkle lights and decor by you two.

Gal friends on the water polo team.
Guy friends and budding relationships, make your smile beam.

Your outgoing personality will take you far
And you will be an IU star.

A job at the fitness center, too.
Football tailgating fun on top of all else you do.
The horizons are endless for you.

(Nineteen poetry lines for her nineteenth year)

Enjoy the last of your teen years.
Happy nineteenth birthday cheers.
Shelby, October 28, 2019

Shining Star

S hining Star in your Sports, inner Self, and work at School,
through out your life will always be your rule.

H elping and Hard working, in times of need
with friends, animals, and your family.

E xcitement, Enthusiasm, high Energy
in everything you do, is what we see.

L oving heart, Listening ear, Learning mind,
Leading others, Laughing spirit, always kind.

B eautiful face, Breath taking smile,
Big dark brown eyes, will take you a mile.

Y outhful spirit will take you far in life, clearly.
Stay your sweet self and know
Tanny and Pappy love you dearly.

Happy eighteenth birthday
Shelby, October 28, 2018

B

She's Seventeen

Material for a beauty queen.
Toned, muscular, and very fit
From working out more than a little bit.

Fun to watch her gymnastic cheerleading.
Her flips keep your heart rapidly beating.
Posts with friends and events on Instagram
Keep us updated and saying *Shazam!*

Fashionable outfits and hairdos on any day
Give her that *Shelby charm* in every way.
She's smart and makes excellent grades.
She's college bound as plans get made.
Child care job and school internship,
She had fun with Tanny taking a swimming dip.

And deep within her heart
There is that giant part,
Loving goodness from within
That shines forth in her beautiful grin.

The only thing better than her beautiful face
Is when she gives hugs and loving grace.
Love for family, friends, and stray dogs,
Makes her a beacon in any fog.

Kind, helpful, compassionate, and sweet,
Happy birthday, Shelby. Hope you have a special treat.
October 28, 2017

Twelfth-Year Memories

Memories of sunglasses and ceramics at the mall.

You trying on clothes and fancy heels, looking so tall.

Gymnastic cheer leading stunts that take my breath away.

Splits, black flips, jumps, and practicing every day.

Swimming fun and playing in the sand.

Learning new braids, always lending a helping hand.

Smiling, caring, and smart as can be.

Technology whiz, helping Pappy and me.

First-born grandchild, not so long ago.

And now you're twelve years old. Where did the years go?

S weet, Super Smart Star

H elpful, Healthy

E nergetic

L ovable, Loving

B eautiful Blessing

Y outhful

Shelby, October 28, 2012

Heart

When Jesus sent you to us, we loved you from the start.
You were such a ray of sunshine from heaven to our heart.

Not just another baby, for since the world began,
God had a special purpose for you in His plan.

That's why he made you special! You're the only one of your kind!
So as you wear this *heart necklace*, keep this in your mind:

The right side of the heart is *God's love for you*,
Each hour of every day your whole life through.

The left side is the *love from your family, friends, Tanny, and Pappy*
And all those blessings in your life that make you very happy.

The point of the heart is to always point you
Toward the *loving purpose God planned for you to do.*

Happy thirteenth birthday.
May this be the start of your amazing teen years and all you do.

Love always,
Pappy and Tanny

This grandmother, in an attempt to keep things equal with grandchildren, sent this same poem to all four granddaughters, Shelby, Taylor, Ella, Olivia, with a heart necklace for their thirteenth birthday.

Special Purpose

Now you're turning sixteen. It happened too fast.
You were such a darling little girl. We just
wanted those years to last.

You know we'll always be here to adore and love you so.
No matter where your future takes you or anywhere you go.

These next years will be exciting as you study and finish high school.
And get your Driver's License, please drive
carefully and obey the rules.

Your sports will bring you pleasure and keep you healthy and strong.
I'm sure you'll set new records, as you speedily run along.

As your great-grandfather often said to me,
Always stay your sweet self. That's the best way to be.

There will be trials and temptations, of that you can be certain.
Always do the right thing and then you won't be hurting.

Fulfill your dreams, live your mission, whether
in Costa Rica or Bloomington.
Charity and outreach are what you'll do
'cause helping others is never done.

Happy sixteenth birthday, Taylor. Always keep that beautiful smile.
That and your good heart will help you go the extra mile.

God be with you as you go that extra mile.
Taylor, March 26, 2018

Shining Star Number Two

I was working out in spandex and tennis shoes.
My phone rang, I answered the call.
A baby is about to be born, gather all.
Taylor Renee Storm was born that day
Her cuteness melted your heart, what more can I say?
She loved food and stroller rides.
Loved to be rocked to sleep to avoid cries.
A photo of her beautiful face framed by curly hair would be
Displayed in photographer's window for all to see.
Naturally athletic, she tried a variety of sports over the years.
She was successful, determined, hard working, without fears.
She tried soccer, swimming, baseball, riding horseback,
Gymnastics, volleyball, and track.

Free spirit, without a care.
Special friends, fun times together to share.
Family fun, grandparent trips and visits.
Loving, caring, compassionate, lifting one's spirits.
Scoliosis surgery, her lemons to squeeze,
She fought hard to rehab, making lemonade, if you please.
Body pain almost ended her position on her track team
Gluten-free diet has improved her physical health, it would seem.
She has proven that no matter what life sends her way,
She will find a solution to do life her special way.
Grateful for her blessings, accepting who you are,
Has made Taylor a mature, young lady, shining star.

Scholastic excellence, athletic awards,
Acceptance to Indiana University her rewards.
Happy eighteenth birthday, Taylor Renee Storm.
Best wishes as you apply for your IU dorm.

Sorry the virus is keeping us apart.
I feel a deep sadness in my heart.
Know we are so proud of you
And the choice you made to protect us two.
We will miss all the activities you were planning to do,
And know you are disappointed, too.
Not being able to run track has brought you strife,
But we are excited to see you run the rest of your life.
Taylor, March 26, 2020

Super at Seventeen

F irecracker, Famous nickname, for your July Fourth birthday.
R espectful and patriotic in every way.
I nterested in playing sports, attending games, knowing the facts.
E xceptional grandson, making conversation, Easy going, to be Exact.
N eatly dressed, Nifty tennis shoe collection for his feet.
D edicated to being a Dependable friend, Determined athlete.
S trong, Spectacular bonds with his *friends*.

COVID-19, school classes on line, unusual year.
Crazy way to end your Sophomore career.
Looking forward to your Junior year at South High School
Fall sports, activities, driver's license, cool.

Memories of football games,
Those intense workouts were insane.
Pappy's dream come true
Of being on the football field to watch you.
Tanny's dream of seeing you tall and strong in all you do.
Physically and character wise, too

Lunch and great conversation downtown
Made Pappy and Tanny smile, not frown.
Your visit at Christmas for Florida sun.
Relaxing and family fun.
Basketball games before the virus quarantine began.
And now seventeen, grown into a *super young man*.

We are proud of who you are and excited about all you do.
We will always adore and very much love you.
Jackson, may you have a super at seventeen birthday.
As you blow out your candles, may your
wishes come true in a special way.
Jackson, July 4, 2020

Sensational Sixteen

J ackson means, *God has been gracious, has shown favor to you.*
  Jacksons are strong, athletic, and modest, too.
A uto license is in your future year.
  Prayers for you to always safely steer.
C onsiderate, caring, and kind,
  Your friends are supportive and of the same mind.
  Coming or going to hang or spend the night,
  You and your friends are always polite.
K nee pain caused by football injury.
  You worked hard to rehab after your surgery.
  Knowingly given lemons, you made lemonade.
  That shows of what you are made.
S trong will, supportive parents. You're going to HS at South!
  Football and basketball teams, cheers from every mouth.
O verly difficult workouts during summer break.
  Discipline, perseverance, determination, drive they take.
  Football practice, working hard.
  Sure that will help you gain an extra yard.
  Weight room toughness, nose to the grind.
  Mental focus, it will help you find.
  You've risen to meet the heat.
  To prove you can't be beat.
N ew school, new friends, new chapter in your story.
  New challenges you will conquer to bring you glory.

I saw the thirteenth year poem I sent under your desktop glass.
  How quickly you've grown up. How quickly the years pass.

You turn sixteen years old today.
We remember how special you are in many ways.

Happy sixteenth birthday.
Jackson, July 4, 2019

Firecracker Fifteen

Happy fifteenth birthday. What can we say?
Today is definitely a firecracker, July fourth, birthday.
As one year ends in your life story.
Another begins with even more glory.

We look forward to your football days
And watching you run those winning plays.
Your hard work at practice will be worth it,
To avoid tackles and be taken down with a hit.

Let's hope Bloomington North has a positive season.
Scoring touchdowns will be the reason.
You will be an asset to your football team,
Because you are tall, quick, lean, and mean.

Then basketball will be your game.
And for your team you will make a name.
Your height will help you raise the score
So your team can be champions once more.

Your passion for schoolwork and good grades,
An unforgettable scholar will be made.
Just know we treasure fond memories of your past.
Can't believe fifteen years have gone by so fast.

Just seems like yesterday
Your Dad did a backflip at the hospital to say:
I have a son, born today.
He is perfect in every way.

Jackson, don't ever forget how much *we love you.*
In the coming year, we look forward to sharing your victories, too.
Jackson, July 4, 2018

Now I'm a Teen

Happy thirteenth. What can we say?
This year is a, *now I'm a teen,* birthday.

As one chapter ends in your life story,
Another begins with even more glory.

As your teen years start,
Keep the following in your heart:

Love for your family, both near and far
They will always think of you as their star!

Trust in God's ways to help you steer,
Your choices will be ever clear!

Passion for schoolwork, music, sports each day,
You'll grow into the best young man in every way!

Tanny and Pappy wish we could be there today
To help you celebrate in a special way.

Just know we treasure fond memories of your past.
We can't believe thirteen years have gone by so fast.

As you become a teen, don't forget how much we love you.
We look forward to the next chapter of your teen years, too.

Happy thirteenth birthday
Jackson, July 4, 2016
JT, June 30, 2018

Joshua Tyler

J oshua means leader, generous, savior
who shows exemplary behavior.

f O otball is a favorite sport for which he was made
and he will help his team excel in eighth grade.

S portsmanship, scholarship, and sense of humor are
important to him, he always raises the bar.

H oops, as in basketball game,
he practices often to improve his aim.

U p early using his chin-up bar.
He will someday be an exercise star.

A rtistic, creative, designer of athletic shoes.
This boy has energy, hard for him to snooze.

T wo, as in Big two card game played with family.
He is often the champion, as Pappy is unhappy to see.

Y outhful, yet mature, for his age.
Exceeds others who are at this same life stage.

L oving, likable, loyal to friends and family.
In cards, he is lucky as lucky can be.

E xercising for a stronger body and six pack.
Muscle definition he does not lack.

R espectful to all, always ready to roll.
Most responsible fourteen-year-old we know.

*Happy fourteenth birthday
Joshua Tyler, JT, June 30, 2019*

Fearless at Fifteen

JT Storm, as his new sport, has taken up tennis.
Forehand, backhand, serve, he does not miss.
His coach at school got him started.
To improve he is whole hearted.
Florida Spring Break opportunity,
Tennis lessons with Pro Palo it would be.

Every stance he was shown, positions for better play,
JT Storm kept hitting to perfection that day,
He hit cross-court returns, down-the-line tennis shots.
As he follows through, shots are *smokin'* hot.
He's learning how to use that racquet.
So watch out when he charges the net.

During COVID-19, all school work diligently completed.
Challenging workouts daily repeated.
Workout schedules assigned for family members.
Posted on the refrigerator so all would remember.

Skateboarding seems to be another interest.
Looks like JT is trying his best
To get his skateboard airborne for Ollie tricks
And his action, sport fix.
At Big two card game, for numbers, fabulous memory.
JT loves to win, especially beating his Pappy.

You have in place those qualities to be successful,
To have a life that's essentially special.
Scholar, athlete, trustworthy son.
Watch out, world, he's the one.
When he wants something, he gets it done.
Fearless at fifteen, our fabulous grandson!
JT, June 30, 2020

Sweet Sixteen, Sophomore Scene

So now you're turning sixteen. It happened all too fast.
Guess we just wanted those little girl years to last.
But you've turned into such an amazing teen,
We can't wait. What's in this next year's scene?

These next years will be exciting as you study and finish high school.
Get your Driver's License, please drive carefully and obey the rules.
Your sports will bring you pleasure and keep you healthy and strong.
I'm sure you'll set some records as your
volleyball team moves along.

You will enjoy your friends and the fun things you like to do.
Homecoming activities, new adventures, and special trips, too.
Family fun, weekends at the cabin with boat or bow and arrow,
You just love the out doors in spring, summer, fall, or winter snow.

You know we'll always be here to adore and love you so.
No matter where your future takes you or anywhere you go.
You were that miracle baby, so special and sweet.
Watching you grow up has been a tremendous treat.

As your great-grandfather often said to me,
Always stay your sweet self. That's the best way to be.
There will be trials and temptations, of that you can be certain.
Always do the right thing and then you won't be hurting.

God has a special life purpose that He wants you to find.
That's why He made you unique, you're the only one of your kind.
Fulfill your dreams and laugh each day
And do your Sophomore year your way.

Happy sixteenth birthday, Ella. Always keep that beautiful smile.
That and your good heart will help you go the extra mile.
Ella, October 10, 2019

From Playhouse to Tree Blind

Happy fifteenth birthday. This poem is sent to say
Today is definitely a special October birthday.
As one year ends in your life story,
Another begins with even more glory.

We look forward to your volleyball days,
And hearing about those winning plays.
Your hard work at practice will be worth it,
When you score with a dig or great hit.

Let's hope you have a fun season
Doing your best will be the reason.
You will be an asset to your team.
You are tall, quick, smart, and lean.

Then hunting will be your game,
Sitting in a tree blind, staying warm and sane.
It will be fun to see what you bag or shoot,
More trophies for your wall to boot.

Your passion for school work and good grades,
An unforgettable scholar will be made.
Choices to decide about your future
And your life work as you mature.

Just know we treasure fond memories of your past.
Can't believe fifteen years have gone by so fast.
We drove to the hospital, an hour away,
Your parents were so excited and did say,

We have a daughter, born today.
She is perfect in every way.

Just seems like yesterday,
Let's play house and color, is what you would say.
Don't forget how much, *we love you.*
And look forward to sharing this year's victories, too.
Ella, October 10, 2018

Let Love Win

When you were a little girl, you liked to play dress-up,
With fancy dresses, funny hats, pretty dishes, and tiny tea cups.

As you grew up, those fancy clothes were left in a box,
Instead you wore a school backpack, new shoes, and cool socks.

A bow and arrow were your game.
Hunting and tree blinds kept you sane.

Dedication and hard work made for success at school.
Your sweet and loving personality was like the Golden Rule.

Soccer and volleyball team fun,
With your healthy body, you have already won.

As we grow, we soon know that life is not always easy.
We cross paths with people whose lives are anything but breezy.

Whether a teacher, friend, or team mate,
It is always a chance and choice to show how we rate.

I think God gave us a heart
So when life seems to come apart,

The love that is stored deep inside
Will overflow the ebbing tide.

That love is always greater
Than fear, sadness, and anger.

So on your birthday I hope you know
Life has an ebb and flow.

It is our job to stay afloat
And climb back in our boat.

Let love from your family
And from Tanny and Pappy,

Let love win each day,
No matter what anyone will say.

Ella, know in your heart
You are growing up to do your part.

Always be your sweet self each day
And win the world with your smiling way.

Extra special is what I hope your fourteenth birthday will be.
Have some extra ice cream and cake for Pappy and me.
Ella, October 10, 2017

My granddaughter experienced bullying at
school, thus my reference to life coming apart
and crossing paths with breezy people.

Remembering Summer Fun

Diving for rings and sticks while swimming at White Eagle pool,
Going down the slide and looking real cool.
Making sister Livy look like a mermaid, buried in the sand,
So completely covered, couldn't see her hand.
Summer cousin fun at the water park,
Slipping and sliding until almost dark.

Helping Pappy pick vegetables from the garden each day,
Zucchini bread was always baking away.
Biking around our neighborhood,
Enjoying the outdoors, best we could.
Paddle boating at the River Walk lake,
Photos of the Bell Tower, ducks, us eating ice cream, we did take.

Playing with the new dolls was lots of fun,
Especially taking photos of them in the flowers, trees, and sun.
Dressing up and eating at the club for dinner,
The strawberries and cookies were always a winner.
Shopping for school supplies, tennis shoes, and new outfits,
Back packs, yellow sticky notes, and other tidbits.

Watching *Frisbee Dog Tricks* at the dog show,
As off to Oberweis for more ice cream we would go.
Practicing tennis and chasing the ball,
But using the backboard was best of all.
Other things I remember are the mall merry-go-round,
Miss Michele's Cake Pops and how easily they went down.

Ella, hope you have a wonderful ninth birthday!
And get to celebrate in a special way.
Go shopping and spend your birthday money.
Get something special to you, Honey.
Ella, October 10, 2012

New Books

Dearest Olivia,

Hope you received your new books to read.

Sent to wish you a *happy birthday* indeed.

Please enjoy them while your ankle mends.

Get well soon wishes Pappy and Tanny do send.

Hope your *twelfth birthday* is a special day

And you get to celebrate in a fun way.

We miss you but you are always close at heart

Even though we live so far apart.

So lots of birthday wishes from Tanny and Pappy.

Have a wonderful day and make it snappy.

Hugs and kisses from Florida

Olivia, March 28, 2017

What? No Poem

What? No poem for your birthday? What was I thinking?
I remember searching for a cute top that was the perfect fitting.

I took pictures of several tops, sending photos to your Mother.
She replied, *Yes,* to one, to the second
and third, *Please try another.*

Since you and Taylor were the first and
second family birthdays of the year,
Just happened you both got packages
to open, you far, she was near.

Never gave poems a thought until I sent
money, no cards or gift to mail.
Ella did get both, her special *turning teenager* birthday to hail.

So please forgive Tanny! The last thing I want to do,
Is make you feel left out and sad too.

Pappy and I do not have favorites, but want each one of you
To feel special and loved because of your unique self too.

No poem for *hunter* Ella who fired only *one* shot,
To bring down a buck on the spot.

No poem for Mom, even though she *works hard* for the family,
And is always there for whatever you need her to be.

No poem for Dad, even though he is the *glue*
That holds your family together, too.

So, Olivia, here is a poem just for you today
Because there are always so many things we want to say!

You were that special surprise gift from God, that was so neat
And made the Kuper family complete.

Watching your grow and learn brought joy and wonder to all,
As your vocabulary, reading, and creativity kept us in awe!

Your musical talents: piano, percussion, playing songs by ear,
Performing piano recitals and school concerts, so dear.

Hearing music in your head to a special beat,
A song writing musician in the making, so neat.

Mathematical magic you seem to possess
As you solve difficult problems and ace your tests.

Reading books seems to be your joy and delight,
As you rapidly read through volumes day and night.

Winning awards and honors with your artistic projects,
Detailed creativity and delightful designs they reflect.

Mind Crafting, home work projects, you giving more than your best.
Not stopping until you know your expectations
are better than the rest.

But even though you have so many amazing qualities,
We simply love you for your unique personality.

Making friends has always been your special gift.
Your caring nature gives those around a confident lift.

Sweet, loving, kind, helpful, smart, and bright,
You are a star sending out light.

We always enjoy hearing about your life
And want you to be happy and without strife.

So hope this poem catches you up to the rest.
And makes you feel like you are the best.
Olivia, December 25, 2017

Just For You

Olivia,
Your birthday gift is hidden
Somewhere in your house.

So you will have to find it
And be sneaky as a mouse.

The gift is *not* on the first floor.
You must go upstairs.

It is *not* in the room
Where you brush your hair.

It is *not* in a bedroom
Painted purple or blue,

But in a place where
Your Mother puts her shoe.

We hope you like your present!
We picked it *just for you.*

It's hidden with lots of love!
From Pappy and Tanny, too

Olivia, March 28

I don't remember the gift, but I do remember how much fun Olivia
always had solving riddles and searching for hidden treasures.
The teacher in me was helping her practice negative attributes.

Fifteen, Math and Music Queen

It's your birthday, and you now turn fifteen.
You're our accomplished math and music queen.

Music extravaganza your Freshman year.
Playing the marimba, you had no fear.
Musical skills tested for a grade,
By a panel of staff to be made.
Excellence, competence to compete,
Precision, rhythm, your perfect beat.

All the early and late practice hours,
For perfection satisfaction to aspire.
Mom's video, did you ever dream
You would be playing, in that scene?
We are amazed by the music you make
And excitedly await the path you take.

Your math problems are way beyond our skill,
And often make us feel *over the hill*.
You enjoy working number problems
From a challenging curriculum.
Teacher thinks you should be an engineer,
Just listen and let your own heart steer.

You love a blanket while reading books,
Snuggling to relax in your chosen nook.

Then you're in your own little world, too.
And could stay there the entire day through.
Studying hard for good grades at school,
Earning all A's is your golden rule.

Olivia, what we adore most about you,
Loving, caring, considerate, too.
Sense of humor, sharing what you know,
Your excitement about how far you can go.
You're a good friend and enjoy taking care of your pets.
Have a happy fifteenth birthday, you bet.
Olivia, March 28, 2020

Happy Birthday Presents, Jackson

A journal with lots of pages
To record memories of Capstone stages.

Pens, pencils, colored pencils too,
Markers that will not bleed through.

A pencil sharpener and post-it notes
That will fit into the zipper bag to serve as a tote.

Soft-fabric, Heritage Oaks logo, T-shirts, Pappy's favorite,
A new golf hat for the Arkansas sun. Hope all are a perfect fit.

Your schedule shows you have full days,
Meaningful activities in many ways.

We think about you every day,
Love you so much, we want to say.

Work hard, we know you can do it.
So you feel better and be more fit.

Life is a journey, never easy.
But then who said it would be breezy?

We know you are strong, sending prayers for your wellness.
Wearing your new tees and hat you will look stupendous.

Sorry we are all away.
Have a great *seventeenth* birthday, your way.
Jackson, July 4, 2020

Birthday Threads

Create my Tapestry

One thread, friends remembered along the way.
One thread, family across the miles to stay.
Poems written because I wanted to say,
Happy birthday, in my special rhyming way.

Family And Friends

Interesting, colorful tapestry threads,
Friends loved as through life I tread.
Supportive, consistent tapestry threads,
Family members who also led.

Lovely Lady, Beautifully Adorned

Happy eightieth birthday to my special friend, Aileen.
Driving together, each Wednesday night, we can be seen
In my GMC Yukon, I uber her,
But riding in her Mustang, I do prefer.

We share our joy for singing.
Our music we will be bringing.
As sopranos in our church choir,
Always trying the next note higher.

We never run out of things to say,
To St. John's Church, we chat all the way.
We share our joys and our concerns,
Our challenges and heart's yearns.

Prayer requests and plans we make,
Even a special recipe we bake.
All the big and little happenings in our life,
Our praises, prayers, and our strife.

Through times of surgery and rehabbing,
Delicious meals you were bringing.
Your cards and thoughtful gifts,
Gave me a healing, spiritual lift.

We watch for deer grazing in Misty Creek,
Miss the entrance gentleman with whom we liked to speak
I enjoy seeing their beautifully manicured yard
And know it's because of Tom's working hard.

Aileen has fun playing cards with her friends.
Great stories, of their special relationships, have no end.
Her hair is always perfectly set.
She's the loveliest, beautifully adorned lady I've ever met.

Their fabulous, living room Christmas tree,
Decorated with hundreds of glass ornaments for all to see.
Each ornament has an interesting story
That gives the holiday tree extra glory.

In the family room, is another, unique tree,
Decorated with bears and a bear collection to see.
Now a master bathroom completely renovated.
After many months, that room has been beautifully updated.

All this makes their home a comfortable castle,
A fun place for family and a haven from life's hassle.
We share our strong faith and love,
Our family ties and answers to prayers from God above.

Hope this is one of your happiest birthdays.
You are so special in so many ways.
Aileen, November 4, 2019

Happy Seventy-second Birthday, Alan

Life now can be very distressful.
Hope your special day is restful.
Past memories are fun to recall:
Awards for church league Fantasy Football.
Humorous dialogue at Darrell's Barbecue,
Organized and run especially by you.
Geckos for a lunch bite to eat,
Football widows could meet and greet.

Sunday morning, after church to chat,
Ball team scores, who was at bat,
Waiting for Cindy to leave the Welcome Center
After she has provided for every member.
Deciding on a place for brunch,
Where we can talk and crunch.

Afternoon library concert, surprising delight.
Daiquiri Bar drinks before dinner that night.
San Marcos, Venice, an Italian dinner,
Perfect ending, a delicious winner.
Under a street lamp, a foursome photo,
Taken with our special beaux.

A Thanksgiving Feast celebration,
Time to be grateful for friends occasion.
Cindy's homemade sweet potato dish,
Was heavenly and very delish.
Valentine Day dinner at Potter's Place
Wine, poems, love, embrace, grace.

Movie Group with popcorn treats,
Movies to watch and then critique.
Men's Retreat planned and organized.
Your goals and commitment prioritized.
FL Studio Theatre, *Bright Star* play,
Music and acting fabulous, we did say!

So special friend, have a fabulous birthday.
Celebrate in your own creative way.
Alan, March 28, 2020

From Minnesota To Sarasota

Hope you have a happy birthday.
Extra special in many ways.
Enjoy your hammock on your lanai.
Eat ice cream, cake, or your favorite pie.

Have fun with Boogie and Sota walking,
Showing off your baby, with friends talking.
Pushing your new doggie stroller.
Sota looking adorable with blond fur.

Blow out your candles, one by one,
Making a wish for all things fun.
Your new villa on golf hole three
Will begin holding exciting memories.

You've had a very busy year,
Appalachian Trail, showing no fear.
Boating, canoeing, hiking new trails,
Uphill, downhill, mountain tops and dales.

Minnesota summer and early fall
Moving from condo to villa—not always a ball.
May Sota learn to settle in,
So your life will soon be a win.

May you live this coming year happily,
Surrounded by good friends and family.
Happy birthday
Annie, November 22, 2019

Annie's husband is an avid golfer, hence the name Boogie, one shot over par on a golf hole. The new puppy, is named after the last part of the words Sarasota and Minnesota.

Together Across the Miles

To my best friend on her special day,
Happy fortieth. What more can I say?

I've known you for almost half your life years.
We've shared our hopes, our dreams, and our fears.

I'm reminded of your concern, support, caring,
Your love, interest, kindness, and sharing.

Pregnancies, babies, watching our ladies grow.
What life had in store, little did we know.

New Year Eve's parties, ball games in the sun.
Every weekend card games and Hi Li Swim Club fun.

Visiting us when we moved away.
Seeing the sights by night and day.

So many fond memories I have of you.
Just wish I could be there to celebrate, too.

Although we're separated by so many miles,
I still send you laughter, joy, and smiles.

I hope this fortieth birthday is fabulous for you.
And that you have a wonderful year, too.
Barbara, November 18, 1986

Incredible Seventy

Happy seventieth birthday wishes I send
For Barbara, my dearest lifelong friend.
Early marriage years, softball fun,
Long night games or days in the sun.
Babies born, exciting watching them grow,
Playing outside or sledding in the snow.

We swapped baby sitting for your bowling.
You watched the ladies play, while I went skating.
Memories of card playing nights,
Pop corn, snacks, and other good bites.
Hours spent watching the guys play ball.
Hours talking and missing the umpire's call.

Visiting when we moved away.
Time together, never a long enough stay.
Sharing the ups and downs of life,
And the challenges of being a good wife.
Our spiritual connection was always there,
Giving us hope, when there was despair.

Knowing the other kept us in prayer,
Always made life easier to bear.
And when life had no reason or rhyme,
We knew the other would listen and give us time.
Understanding, accepting, sharing, a big hug and smile.
You, my friend, have always gone the extra mile.

Seventy years, it seems so impossible,
Because you are still so incredible.

Hope your day has extra joy in store,
And birthdays ahead will be many more!
Barbara, November 18, 2016

Barb and Jim visited us in Indianapolis. We went to a Pacers basketball game. Barbara and I were surprised when the game ended. A man seated behind us said, *I can't believe they talked through the entire game. Best friends catching up.*

B A S I A (Polish for Barbara)

B irthday happiness to our dear Basia.

A lways, every day walking her husky, Natasha.

S oul full of thoughtfulness and grace.
    Everyone loves her beautiful, smiling face.

I nterested in improving her putting and golf game
    and trying something new like Goat Yoga—insane.

A lways fashionably stylish
    clothing, jewelry, shoes, handbag, *cute dish.*

G enerous with her friends—
    for her love and help there are no ends.

E nergetically exercising her special routines.
    She can often be seen on fitness machines.

N ewly remodeled and decorated Patio home, too
    sheer window blinds, panoramic patio screen view,

T eaching other how to play Mah-Jongg, and,
    showing them what it means to be a *Joker Slut.*

R eads on a Kindle her many books,
    shares her magazines so others can look.

Year older, wait that can't be true
She doesn't look a day over fifty-two!

Did someone suggest a healthy salad instead of a cake please?
Don't forget the grapes and Goat Cheese.
Happy sixty-sixth birthday.
Basia, May 1, 2016

I've known my Kentucky friend Barbara for fifty-two years. After retiring to Sarasota in 2015, it was not a coincidence to make another new best friend named Basia, which is Polish for Barbara.

Like a Sister

Basia Dear,
Whether we are on our yoga mat
Exercising so we won't get fat,
Or looking for that perfect thing at a festival of art
To make our home look tastefully smart.

Or shopping for clothes or jewelry to wear,
Giving advice on cutting our hair,
Or dining and *wine-ing* and trying new places.
We are determined to cover all restaurant bases.

Playing Mah-Jongg and hoping for a Joker,
While admiring your unique, necklace choker.
Bam, Dot, Crack, Red, North become our pitch
So we can claim *Slut* or *Bitch*.

Seeing you walking with David and Natasha when I'm out.
Always a big smile, wave, asking what I'm about.
No matter what we seem to do
It's always fun being with you.

This new friend has become like a Sister
And when she leaves town I realize how much I *mist-her*.
Basia, you are always there to listen to problems or strife,
It's been such a joy having you in my life!
Happy sixty-seventh birthday to you.
May all your dreams come true.
Basia, May 1, 2017

You Have A Gift

For making people smile,

For going that extra mile,

For caring how others feel,

For being so warm and real,

For knowing just what to say,

For lighting up every day,

For cheering dreams from the start,

For living with so much heart.

So grateful you have a gift.

Thank you for the spirits you lift.

Happy sixty-eighth birthday.

Basia, May 1, 2018

Acrostic Happy Birthday Poem

B irthday is the day after mine.
    Brunch together after church, fun to dine.

E mails sent to make me laugh and smile.
    Always going the extra mile.

C reative, unique, one-of-a-kind greeting cards designed
    Sent to celebrate or cheer those confined.

K ey Chorale practices and concerts over the years.
    Church choir anthem practice, prayers for no fears.

I learned Latin, for a music score, with your teaching.
    We enjoy church choir anthem practice singing.

E xtra special to her Spanish family.
    Extra caring to my spouse and me.

Beckie, happy eightieth birthday.
Hope it is special in every way.

Be safe and avoid COVID-19.
Glad we are ending the quarantine.
Beckie, June 4, 2020

Special Friend
Across the Street

It was 1989 when we first met.
You were the lady with Sadie and later Cinders for a pet.
My special friend across the street
Who would later surprise us with Carrot Cake goodies to eat.

Your two darling daughters, Amy and Megan, who played outside,
Were little and cute with colored chalk on the drive.
Your husband, Jeff, shared the same passion as mine.
GOLF, and it was never enough to just play nine.

We were golf widows together when off they would go.
Later to wine and dine at the Club as their awards did show.
You worked hard for White Eagle so there was justice for all,
At school, the community and the homeowners' hall.

And many events found you involved,
So others could have fun as the years evolved.
You took care of your home, your yard, and the dog's stash,
Sponge painted, tulips planted, and took out the trash.

You mothered, trained, and cared for your girls, two,
As we watched in wonder at how well they grew.
You were involved in their schoolwork every day,
And supported them in sports in your special way.

I've visited your beautiful California dream home on the hill.
The drive to Pebble Beach and Carmel I remember still.
We've shared the ups as well as the downs.
We've shared the smiles as well as the frowns.

We've shared *Women are from Venus and Men are from Mars.*
We've shared our hopes and dreams on the stars.
We've traveled around the world to visit Hawaii,
With luau, shopping, lunching, and new sights to see.

Sailing, snorkeling, special dining each night
At incredibly breathtaking places. What a sight.
The house we rented, with pool in the back.
Leis at the airport, we had nothing to lack.

How the years tick quickly away
But leave behind fond memories in our hearts to stay.
So many events and moments from the past
Linger in our minds forever to last.

And so to my special friend who is *fifty today,*
I just wanted to take this opportunity to say
Happy birthday, Carolyn. May all your dreams come true.
Happy birthday, Carolyn. May blessings continue for you.

As one chapter ends and a new one starts,
We wish for you health and happiness
from the bottom of our hearts,
Carolyn, March 5, 2005

Welcome to the Seventies Club

I've been told it's a special birthday.
Perfect time for all of us to say,
Thank you for the many things you do
And for the times you're there for us, too.
Time on committees, working to show
A better life for all in the HO.
Improving the food service and meals,
Making sure everyone gets the best deals.
Hours spent going the extra mile,
Planning entertainment that brings smiles,
Arranging events for Ladies Night fun,
Organizing golf outings in the sun.
Restaurant options for movie night,
Variety spots for a tasty bite.
Tickets purchased on your cell phone,
Seating for a good theater zone.
Thinking ahead for Venice play tickets.
Mama Mia and Menopause, awesome, you bet.
Discovering new dining pleasures.
Char always knows the latest treasures.
Arranging for Heritage Oaks, plenty of seats,
With a great view that can't be beat,
Ed Smith Stadium, May Pops Concert,
But dinner first, followed by dessert.
Vocal artists, fabulous symphony,
Fireworks to follow for all to see.
Your trips inspire us to travel more.
Your landscaping and villa we adore.

Your energy we wish we had.
Please don't stop being in charge or we will be sad.
Happy birthday to a unique, special lady
Who has given so much so we could be,
Enriched, entertained, satisfied, dined,
Encouraged, cared for, welcomed with wine.
So here's to the Queen of in the know
The newest and foremost places to go.
May your seventieth birthday year
Be filled with health, happiness, wine, and good cheer.
Happy seventieth birthday.
Char, January 26, 2020

Acrostic Happy Birthday, Foxy Lady

C indy, Classy, Charming, Captivating, Cute as Can be.

I deal, Inviting, It's your birthday, we gather to see.

N ice News, each other's faces, latest happenings.

D azzling, Delightful, Daytime, nighttime, now's the time for singing

Y es, Happy Driveway Birthday to our dear Cindy Caputo.

C indy, Caring friend, there in time of need.

A dored, Attentive to bring ice cream, indeed.

P erfect hostess, delicious meals she shares.

U nselfish, generous in how much she cares.

T errific, Tastefully decorated Sarasota home, the best.

O h, Cindy, always fashionably dressed!

Unusual days, unusual times. Coronavirus, Quarantine rhymes.

Can't birthday party in a home, But can't just stay home alone.

Can't hug or closely dance. Catch the virus, can't take the chance.

Thank you for the Driveway Party, To sing and celebrate Cindy.

Best wishes, birthday hugs and hypes.
May you have plenty of toilet paper, sanitizer, and wipes.

Happy sixty-third
Cindy, April, 17, 2020

B

Happy Sixty-ninth Birthday

Happy birthday, sister dear.
Hope you get birthday wishes far and near.

Excited you are living at Wyndham Court Facility
With a pretty room, I could see.

The art work of Dallas on the walls
That you see walking the halls.
Such interesting decor
For everyone to adore.

Your doctor, nurse, and caring staff
Want you to be happy, make you laugh.

Relax in the outdoor courtyard in the sun
Sounds like a great place for everyone.

Enjoy a Coke, your favorite drink,
Some Chocolate, too, would be great, I think.

Hope you like the activities for the day.
Maybe your new friends will say,

It's your birthday! You are sixty-nine.
We think you are mighty fine.
Hope you have your favorite foods, when you dine.
Connie, April 27, 2020

Acrostic for David

D og walking Natasha, his second love

A lways and forever with Basia, his first love.

V ery dedicated friend in good or challenging times.

I ndianapolis racing friends are still important ties.

D ashing and daring in all aspects of life.

G un range practice with posted bull's-eye targets.

E xercise classes help keep him fit.

N ever far for a listening ear or sports conversation.

T ee it up, let's lower the golf score.

R oad trips in his car for get-away fun times.

Y ear older but still going strong.

Happy birthday, dear friend.
David, March 27, 2019

Happy Seventy-fourth Birthday, David

Hope your special day
Is spent your own way.
And the coming year,
Plenty of your favorite wine and beer.

Sharp shooting practice with friends,
The results are your bull's-eye trends.
Plenty walking time with Basia
And of course with your Natasha.

Golfing strokes that are easy, not hard,
With low numbers on your score card.
Fun golf times with your wife,
Pleasing play with no strife.

Challenging rounds with the guys,
Hope your putting is no surprise.
Keep your putter as vertical as possible.
Hit slightly up on the ball—phenomenal!

Numerous race car events to watch.
No accidents to drive you to drinking scotch.
Exercises to keep you strong
And the men's class to prolong.

Healthy but delicious meals for dining.
For now, probably in your chair reclining.
Hopefully soon you can go out again,
To favorite restaurants with your friends.

Happy birthday, good friend. Stay healthy and well.
Happy birthday, good friend. Hope your day is swell.
David, March 27, 2020

Forty, Someone Said?

ಶ

Forty	I even read.
Forty	That can't be.
Forty	He doesn't look that to me.
But then—	
Forty	years, not old if you're a tree.
Forty	the age I used to be.
Forty	A good score for a golf game
Forty	As long as you shoot the back nine the same.
Forty	Love, a tennis score,
Forty	You win with one point more.
Forty	Exercises at the gym and track.
Forty	Stretches are best for the back.
Forty	Basketball baskets, what a score.
Forty	Laps, what a chore.
Forty	Chords on a guitar he strums.
Forty	Tunes Gene gladly hums.
Forty	Notes, what a range to sing.
Forty	And sporty has a nice ring.
Forty	Winks, a short nap.
Forty	Years, a long rap.
Forty	Plus forty working hours a week.
Forty	Files to do in a streak.
Forty	Phone calls to return.
Forty	Operations to learn.
Forty	Would be eight, *Texas Two Steps*, on the dance floor.
Forty	Candles on a cake. Please, no more.
Forty	Minutes, a nice walk in the sun.
Forty	Minutes and the steak is too done.
Minus *Forty*	Degrees in Naperville is rather nippy.
Forty	Inches could be rather hippy.

Forty   Inches could be very busty.

Forty   WD if it's rusty.

Forty   Sexy women, what a treat.

Forty   Dates in a row, a record to beat.

Forty   The age at which life begins, some say.

Forty   The age Gene turned on this past Wednesday.

Forty   Sounds good to me.

Forty   Just the age to be.

Forty   That's pretty nifty.

Forty   sounds better than fifty!

        Gene

Via Text

Linda: Happy birthday, Harry, on this your special day.
       Hope you are having fun with family in every way.
Harry: Thank you in no small part
       From every aspect of my heart.
       Your birthday wishes sent through this vessel
       Mean so much from RP and Linda Messel.
Linda: Two poets, a dangerous pair,
       We always have a rhyme to spare.
       A gift awaits in your villa,
       When you return to Sarasota.
       Ron gone to see his muscle activation guy,
       Enjoy your day as I say good-bye.
Harry: Saying good-bye is always sweet sorrow,
       But we shall reunite in the near morrow.
       Looking forward to the villa surprise.
       Am sure my expression will be one with big eyes.
Linda: You win!
Harry: A contest it was not meant to be.
       I am an amateur when compared to thee.
Linda: It's your birthday, you are a winner.
       Now go enjoy your birthday dinner.
Harry: Okey dokey.

Linda: Blow out your candles and do the Hokey Pokey.

Harry: Left foot in, left foot out. Turn it all about, no doubt.

Linda: Did you rhyme when landing on a dime?

On an aircraft, in the ocean afloat?

Or are you just feeling nifty, now that you are over fifty?

Harry: With birthday wishes from my beloved friends,

Feeling emotional and thankful to make amends,

With gratitude and appreciation aplenty.

Did you say fifty? How about seventy?

Linda: Happy birthday, Harry.

Harry, August 23, 2019

My husband left for a two-hour appointment, one Friday afternoon. I was taking advantage of that time to relax after a busy week, when I realized it was Harry's birthday. I quickly text two rhyming lines, thinking that would have to work this year. Maybe a poem next year. Harry text back resulting in the above poem.

Nifty At Ninety

Gloria, many years you've been *Alleluia's Parish Nurse.*
In knowing the best words to say, you are well versed.
I recall Ron recovering from quintuple bypass surgery.
You came to Edwards Hospital, checking his behavior, you see.
Too many visitors in the room, you said.
Recovering patients should be resting in bed.
The *too many visitors* left, Nurse Gloria could see first hand
How Ron was healing, the surgeon's rehab plan.
You and your wise advice were there again for prostate cancer.
You recommended Dale's surgeon, he became Ron's answer.

Alleluia was built on our *Small Group Ministry.*
Getting each member into a group was our goal, you see.
You were there from the start, a Small Group Leader
With encouraging ways to share and be the reader.
No one could monopolize discussion with your *talk stick.*
Moving the stick from person to person did the trick.
As leaders, we would monthly meet for our own lessons.
Practice for our group, pray for all, brainstorm solutions.
For several years my widowed father, Irvin, was in your group.
His Alzheimer's was a challenge for all, but you kept him in the loop.
Every meeting he would take out his wallet,
show the photo of his Phyll,
My mother, the love of his life. *Did I show
you her picture? Miss her still.*

Attended many *Women's Retreats,* over the years, doing your part.
Always caring for others, sharing from your heart.

Those early years we retreated with Our Saviour's, not to be alone.
But as we grew Alleluia, with more members,
we were soon on our own.
Various speakers, affecting our faith, making learning fun,
Time to go outside for fellowship with friends and a walk in the sun.
Meaningful discussions, good food, and lots of conversations.
Private alone time for prayers and self-reflection.

You were always quite the woman, travels taking you far and near.
Loved your voice and humor sharing adventures for all to hear.
Sometimes grandchildren would accompany you on your way
And at various hostels you would stay.
Replaced at the same time, you did both knees.
I know the pain of one knee replaced, you were quite the lady.
Shared the fun you had grooming and riding your own horse,
Spending time in God's great outdoors,
gracious pleasures of course.
Professionally lectured your way through many years.
Helped trained nurses to develop confidence without fears.
Awards and accolades always coming
your way for what you would do.
You were gracious but private about sharing, too

You helped write the history of Alleluia by the way you are living.
Loving, caring, serving, healing, listening, giving, nurturing.
You once advised me, Make the decision
based on what you know today.
Don't second-guess yourself or look back.
Down the road, come what may,
If the facts or situations change, then change your plan as well.
That advice has helped me not get stuck
in indecision, so I feel swell.

As I reflect to make reason and rhyme,
Wisdom shared with many over time,

Such grace along the way.
Don't waste time on guilt any day.
Your voice soothing, whatever you read or say.
Ninety years is a long journey
Lived in an amazing Christian discovery and victory!

Happy ninetieth birthday, Gloria Henderson.
May you have and get anything you want!
Gloria, May 10, 2020

Happy Birthday
To Harry

Thank you for keeping us merry,

Thank you for giving everyone your super smile.

And for always going the extra mile.

New granddaughter helps you celebrate,

Makes this year's birthday extra great.

Harry, August 23, 2017

Jack, Kerry, Harry and Ron

Four men became friends in Sarasota.

They golfed and fished in Minnesota.

They fried fish they caught.

They enjoyed ice cream they bought.

Those four friends who lived in Sarasota.

Three of the friends received a coffee mug for their birthday.

On the side of each mug, a photo of their four mugs, a fun way to say

Have a happy birthday.

Mugs

Have you thought about the meaning of the word *mug*?

Hope you don't have a *mugshot* taken on your birthday,

Nor get *mugged* on the highway,

But your *mug*,

Along with your friends' *mugs*,

On a coffee *mug*,

Will help you feel a *happy birthday hug*.

Jack, July 2, 2019 Kerry, August 2, 2019 Harry, August 23, 2019

The fourth friend is my husband Ron. I still owe him a mug.

Sensational Sixty

We first met at Waubonsie High School in Naperville in 1989.
You were the counselor, oh so kind.
We had moved from California to Naperville
With a Junior named Jennifer and Freshman named Jill.
Jill was unhappy (no, angry) with the move
And decided to rebel so she could prove
How wrong we were to make the move,
How impossible for her to fit the new groove.

You worked with her, you worked with me.
You helped our family see,
How hard the move could be.
The things we could do to help Jill feel free.
You led the *Systematic Training for Effective Parenting* class
That gave new ideas to help each lad and lass.
Learning to take consequences and responsibility,
Finding new ways to be the best you could be.

You prayed with me at *Moms in Touch,*
That brought the strength that helped so much.
Each week we met, school and community concerns did share,
As we tried to help the burden we all had to bear.
A spiritual bond had begun to grow
That would last the years and mean more than you know.
Your strength in faith, yet gentle ways
Would sustain us through difficult days.

God does work in mysterious ways.
During one cold January day,

Howard's new job took him away.
You quickly sold your house, needed a place to stay.
Ron was at Sierra Tucson for counseling,
So you moved in and helped with my healing.
We became roommates and once again
You were there to help with the pain.

A miracle healing of our relationship at last.
When Ron came home, you helped with struggles to get past.
You were our angel, *the best of the best.*
And then you had to leave to move west.
Your car was packed, the top was stacked,
It barely cleared the opening, as out the garage you backed.
Your prayers, your blond hair, your bubbly ways
Would be missed by all, each and every day.

We may be separated by many miles,
But we'll always remember your beautiful smile.
Thank you for being our angel, our light.
Thank you for helping us both day and night.
You are a wonderful counselor, friend so true.
Inspirational author who gave us life anew.
Happy sensational, sixty.
Jeanne Tiffany

Sixty, Someone Said

Sixty, someone said?
Sixty, I think I read.

Sixty's not old if you're a tree.
Sixty, the age we used to be.

Sixty mph in the I-75 slow lane.
Sixty mph especially if you drive in the FL rain.

Sixty, a fabulous golf score.
Sixty ways your cute wife to adore.

Sixty, the perfect age to buy
A Heritage Oaks Villa—oh, my!

Decorated in Coastal Blue,
Cozy, comfortable for you and Michelle, too.

Sixty-plus times you will drive your Green Hornet.
Sixty-plus times we hope you win your golf bet.

Sixty years old, what more can we say?
Sixty years old on your birthday, today.

May your years ahead be filled with friends and family fun,
And lots of loving memories in the Sarasota sun.
Happy birthday.
John, October 21, 2019

A Special Gift For Sharing

Style show outfits for Ron and me.
We had fun, as you could see.
Christmas shopping for the family,
You made perfect choices easy as could be.
All the clothing goodies, with prices great,
Always keeps financially happy, Ron's mate.

The *Send-Off to Cleveland Clinic Surprise Affair*
Was *over-the-top* with your special care.
The basket of goodies with protein bars and treats,
Anti-stress pillow, compression socks, can't be beat.
His and *her* Blue Emu topical cream,
We thought we were having a dream.

A mask for one's eyes to block the light
So one gets a better sleep at night.
Godiva Chocolates and Lifesavers were gone in a blink,
As were the Max Golf Protein Milk drinks.

Danish pastries arrived in the mail,
So much better than a salad with kale.
Pastries delivered to our Cleveland Clinic hotel room,
Suddenly we were all smiles, no more gloom.

Lots of visits once we were home.
Your smile made us feel we were *never alone*.
Birthday surprises and Abel's Ice Cream.
Both delicious flavors made us beam.

How can one person be so sweet,
To every one she meets?
You must have a special gift for caring
And always helping, giving, and sharing.
We love you for all you do
To make us feel special, too.

Happy birthday, Marcie. We hope your day
Is special in every way.
Marcie, June 27, 2018

Memories of Mary

May fifth, Cinco de Mayo, something missing?
Mary's authentic Mexican cuisine.
When she cooked a Mexican dish,
Shopped ingredients at stores where they spoke Spanish.
Always an interesting new recipe for the cooking Queen.
Over the years, we all enjoyed her delicious dinner scenes.
We asked her husband if he could choose, what would be his wish,
He said, Mary has never twice made the same dish.

Mary, Mary, quite the green thumb.
How does your garden grow and overcome
Weather, weeds, too much or too little watering?
With hard work on hands and knees, lots of caring.
Remembering your gorgeous flowers from your yard.
For making full bouquets, you are a die-hard.
Every color, kind, variety, fragrance, you grew
So we could all enjoy their beauty, too.

I think we first met at the White Eagle pool
Swimming our laps to stay healthy, our rule.
You were expecting a baby, soon born, Miss Betsy.
Growing-up daughter years, fun for you and me.
Making a house a home, comfortable, inviting.
Furniture, draperies, paint, accessories, special lighting.
Graduation, college choices, adult life stages,
Daughter's pet, apartments, career and job changes.
Blessings, challenges, family life.
Retirement times for husband and wife.

Remembering many Mary moments, grateful for your friendship.
Thank you for making the years better
through our personal relationship.
Happy birthday. May you have many more years
Of good health, dreams, and plans come true. Cheers.
Mary, June 1, 2020

Mar-gar-et Mar-y

The first time I saw her, she was wearing a snazzy, workout getup.
Her son was running in the yard with Mandy, a golden retriever pup.
We were the new neighbors and soon met her family:
Tom, Margaret Mary, Christopher, Meghan,
Kathleen, Susie, and Tommy.

We've watched each other's family grow and change
Through seasons of sunshine and days of rain.
Graduations, weddings, births of each grandchild.
Her life has been anything but mild.

Baptisms, communions, special birthdays,
Kept her celebrating in different ways.
Father Tommy moving to the Vatican in Rome so far away,
Made sharing the days when he was home special in every way.

Camp Gramps was a fun event,
With grandchildren sleeping outside in a tent.
On a summer night, what a fun way,
As long as the sprinklers didn't rain on the day.

Married to husband Tom for more years than I know,
Traveling the world, being together, seemed to keep them aglow.
Margaret Mary lit more than one candle
at church for the Potter crew.
Her prayers and love, there wasn't anything she wouldn't do.

Margaret Mary thought our granddaughters were adorable.
The granddaughters pronounced her name with five syllables.
All the grandchildren loved visiting her home,
And it didn't matter if Mr. Tom was alone.
He would help the ladies cut paper dolls until. . .
Mar-gar-et Mar-y returned and they got their sugar cookie fill.
At spoiling my grandchildren (and husband) they were not *rookies*,
Margaret Mary always had a supply of her
delicious, world-famous cookies.

Visiting their Florida home made us feel special and cool
With bike rides, walks, and floating on a raft in the pool.
Tom and Ron fishing or golfing each day.
The four of us watching Manatees in the bay.

Margaret Mary has shared many a meal.
Shrimp with Scallops and Turkey with Stuffing were quite the deal.
Dedicated to her extended family,
Yet always time for friends like me.

Faithful friend for twenty-three years,
Sharing pleasures, giving hope for the fears.
Passion for helping others has brought her joy,
As she's shared stories of affecting many a girl or boy.

Spiritually, Margaret Mary's an example
of putting God first in your life.
She is a model friend, grandmother, mother, wife.
We've counted it a blessing to be your neighbor.
And are grateful for so many wonderful memories to savor.

May you feel like a Queen on your *seventy-fifth birthday*.
Enjoy the greetings everyone will say.

May you be surrounded by love like a queen's beautiful gown.
May Tom, Susie, Chris, Kathleen, Ellen, Meghan,
Paul, Christopher, Holly, be your pride-and-joy crown.

But the jewels of the crown will of course be,
Grandchildren: Nora, Lucy, Christopher,
Juliet, Charlie, Lizzie, Maureen, and Mattie.

Happy seventy-fifth birthday
Margaret Mary, March 25, 2012

Pastor Jaime

Happy birthday, Pastor Jaime. What can we say?
Hope you have a fabulous day.
Thank you for your sermons on the *Five Stones*.
Those sermons gave me tools instead of moans.
When *giant troubles* or *Goliaths*, come into my life,
God's word and prayer bring comfort, not strife.
As I worship, I'm challenged to serve.
Stepping out, *using my gifts*, God will help calm my nerves.

Relationships—that's what life's about.
Do your chores with a smile, not a bout.
Treasure your *friends*, they're like family.
By your side, they'll always be.
Be the first to say, *I'm sorry or I love you.*
Every day that's what one should do.

Pastor Jaime, I see you pray.
Give your sermon without notes on Sunday.
Greet and visit members with your smile,
Whether in homes or in the church aisle.
Use humor in all you *do*,
That draws everyone to you.
Your prayers are from the heart,
Inspired by your spirit-filled part.
You certainly have a special way
Of getting your flock to follow through on what you say.

Your outreach to schools to help children read,
Will be a community blessing indeed.
The church is active and alive.
To fulfill God's Kingdom, we see you strive.

Alpha groups and Wednesday night classes,
Great way to engage the masses.
You've made me feel welcome and a part
Of your church, fed my soul and stirred my heart.
Hope you take time to celebrate
Your special birthday date.
Pastor Jaime, October 10, 2016

Pound Cake Queen

Little sister's sixty-eighth birthday.
She's always generous in every way.

Baked pound cakes galore.
Renovated bathroom, glass chandelier, new floor.

Grandkids, her delight.
Star gazing at night.

Hummingbirds on the feeders, wings flapping.
New deck swing, always swinging.

Garden produce canning,
Ceiling fans fanning.

Southern comfort meals.
Travel adventures in a fifth wheel.

Life-long friends on mountain getaways,
Cruising trips for many days.

Washington, D.C. Veteran flights,
Tired, but content at night.

Home care nursing,
Outer Banks relaxing.

Retirement ways,
Busy, fun days.

Birthday wishes,
Please no dirty dishes.

Plenty hugs and kisses,
To the birthday Mrs.

Patty, October 14, 2019

Sixty-five

May your year be filled with:

Lots of movies and good eats,
And all kinds of other unexpected treats.

Health, happiness, and blessings to you,
Good times with friends and family, too.

Fun at your classes and working out,
And relaxing times shopping about.

Plenty of tennis and time on your yoga mat.
Happy sixty-fifth birthday to you, Miss Pat.
Pat N, September 29, 2016

Caring Heart

Your beautiful hair, whether straight or curly,
Makes you always look great, sexy, and girly.
Your bright eyes and winning smile
Always take you that extra mile.

Your loving, listening spirit
Is always inviting when we are near it.
Your nursing knowledge and practical skills
Frequently help us over insurmountable hills.

You were a good friend from the start
And always have a caring heart.
We've had fun at movies and various dining spots,
Playing Mah-Jongg, trying to win the money pots.

Celebrating special occasions in our lives,
Helping out when there are bad vibes.
You love traveling and family fun,
And playing tennis in the Florida sun.

Yoga, exercising, working out,
Riding bikes with Harry, being out and about.
So tonight we celebrate you on your special day.
May next year be filled with good health and getting your way.

May you win your tennis games.
When playing Mah-Jongg, always remain sane.
We wish you a special sixty-seventh year,
As we raise our glasses, drink glasses, that is,
And give you a big, birthday cheer.
May this year bring everything you hold dear.
Pat N, September 29, 2018

Welcome Home

Happy Birthday, Patty. I've missed your curly hair and warm smile.
Seems like you and Harry have been gone a long while.

Exercising without you here,
Wondering what the grandkids were doing to make you cheer.

Mah-Jongg attendees are down to three or four,
Looking forward to when there are more.

Always fun seeing you win and say, *Mah-Jongg!*
Such joy for four dimes is a happy song.

Movies on Tuesday night,
With a delicious dinner quick bite.

Always a fun answer to *What's for dinner?*
Even if the movie is not a winner.

Can't wait, our Tuesday tradition to resume,
To add a spark to our rainy gloom.

Miss our talks, you are always there,
With your special, tender, loving care.

You always offer advice to help
When I feel the need to yelp.

Thank you for your unique friendship!
Welcome home from your long trip.
Patty, September 29, 2019

Belated Wishes, Phil

What? I missed your birthday!
I am in such dismay.

Please accept these late wishes:
For more of life's riches.
From your wife, more kisses.
From your computer, no glitches.
No party as we stay in our niches.
TV watching that enriches.
May you develop no twitches.
Nor any allergic itches.

May you find joy in:
Movie night memories and treats.
Dinners with delicious foods to eat.
Satisfaction from monies raised.
Community service from you, praised.
Hosting gourmet dinners for your friends.
Enjoying their company, their wishes to attend.
Your hospitality to others always transcends.
Good times with golfing buddies.
Better hitting with all your *clubbies*
Putting, chipping, practicing more.
May it improve your golf score.
Memories of all your travels and trips,
Whether by car or cruise ship.

Hope your birthday was extra special.
Health, happiness for next year, essential.
Happy seventy-third birthday
Phil, March 29, 2020

B

Hair Dryer and Scissors

Hair dryer and scissors, tools of your trade.
For being an expert hair stylist, you were made.

You've made me look beautiful these past four years.
My fabulous haircuts, I give you three cheers.

My color, my cut, my special style,
You do whatever it takes, you go the extra mile.

You always look cute wearing the latest fashion.
Talking to and caring for each customer is your passion.

You listen and show concern as a good friend,
Regardless of how much your ear we bend.

Your sparkling eyes and winning smile,
Your pretty outfits always in style.

You have a tattoo and a tan,
You can deal with seventy, I know you can.

Happy birthday, Rochelle.
Hope you get a day off from hair spray and gel.

Happy birthday and may this next year
Bring you health, happiness, and all you hold dear.
Rochelle, October 15, 2018

Welcome

Welcome to the Heritage Oaks family. You bet.
Great to have you close by on Samoset.

Your villa is lovely. We can tell you've worked hard.
Friends coming to visit must be registered
with the gate-house guard.

Thank you for the Open House. It was fun.
Enjoy the calendar photos of Sarasota's setting sun.

Take it to Naperville when you return home.
To remind you to hurry back to Florida when you roam.

Happy belated birthday, we wanted to say.
Won't forget next year as our granddaughter's is the same day.

Rosemary, March, 26, 2019

Sensational Suanne

Was it luck, meant to be, or fate
That we would be Heritage Oaks *roof mates*?
Friendship threads over time, woven tightly
To deal with life challenges mightily.
As I reminisce about this past year,
So many fun memories I hold dear.

How we look forward to every Thursday,
So our group can gather together to play,
Bams, Cracks, Dots, Dragons,
Flowers, Winds, Jokers, Mah-Jongg.
Savory snacks, friends like family.
So reassuring to get together to just be.

Practicing Ashtanga Vinyasa Yoga on our mats any day.
Breathing through Down Dog, Tree Pose, Warrior, Namaste.
Stretching, strengthening, relaxation,
Reiki healing, soul searching meditation.

The amazing Chang plays Dvorak, Sarasota Symphony,
(Old man, next to me, reading a book, head almost to knee.)
Brahms Concerto, Walton's Symphony, Sunday afternoon delight.
(What is that smell? Let's go for dinner tonight.)
Such incredible music, fabulous conducting as well.
Our Symphony, renewing, rejuvenated, inspiring spell.

Inviting villa, new edgy light fixtures, and mirror on bedroom wall,
Black chairs by the dining table, art work in the hall.
Comfortable lanai with candles and fire pit.
Perfect place to relax and just sit.

Happy sixty-eighth birthday to my adorable roof mate.
Hope you have a fabulous day and sometime a date.
Suanne, May 31, 2020

Happy Birthday, Sweet Sue

It's my pleasure to have met and know you.
Seated together, soprano section, St. John's Church Choir,
Always trying for that note that goes a little higher.

Partners in crime in the back row,
Practicing anthems weekly as we go.

Joining hands with others whenever we pray,
In choir or church, our hearts awaiting answers along the way.

We share monthly Movie Group fun times,
With dinner, dessert, movie discussion reason and rhyme.

The Fifties Club to celebrate our marriage years,
We share our blessings, have some cheers.

Night time dinners, brunches during the day
Enjoyable memory at Florida Studio, *Bright Star* play.

You always care about how others are feeling,
Brought a meal to my door during illness dealing, for healing.

Our husbands' Fantasy Football competition for a winner,
With trophy award, and Darrell's delicious Barbecue dinner.

Your beautiful jewelry, hair in perfect place,
Matching outfits, toe ring, pretty, smiling face.

Abe, your daughters, their husbands,
surround you like a Queen's gown.
All those precious grandchildren, the jewels in your crown.

Happy seventeenth, or seventy first.
Love the way the numbers you reverse.
Missing you and the music we rehearse.
Sue, April 6, 2020

Seventy-five Seventy-five Seventy-five

I was afraid to write a poem about your life.
I could not remember the name of your first wife.
But people can read between the lines
Because you are a man so fine.
Anyone reaching seventy-five years,
Deserves remembering memories others hold dear.
Proud parents that January, 1945.
Steve was always so alive.
I'm sure those growing-up years were busy,
Even making your dear parents feel dizzy.
University of Louisville, same time frame.
Steve and Ron didn't know each other's name.
After moving to Chicago, they met.
Business, then pleasure, you bet.
Insurance issues, Steve was always there.
He had the answers and would always care.
Galena and the *peachy* view.
There was always plenty to do.

Dining, exercising, hiking,
Golfing, gambling, or just relaxing.
Chicago dinners, tennis matches to play,
Art festivals and concerts, fun night or day.
Daughters grew up, too quickly it seems.
Life's ups and downs and broken dreams.
But then Bat Mitzvahs and wedding days,
Grandchildren and exciting new ways.
What, Steve has a new wife.
Doris just gave Steve new life.
Doris's life, so full and sweet
Would end too soon—a defeat?
No, No, No!
Doris would want him to continue to go.
So forward with life,
Missing his wife.
Piano lessons, Florida trips,
Glass blowing artistry and golf tips.
Anyone reaching seventy-five years,
Deserves our praises and cheers.
Happy seventy-fifth birthday!
Steve, January, 2020

Eighty

Eighty, someone said?
Eighty, I think I read.
Eighty miles an hour is a fast speed.
Eighty inches of rain is a lot indeed.

Eighty-degree weather can be very warm.
Eighty-miles-an-hour-wind in a strong storm.
Eighty is not a low golf score.
Eighty years old, you want to live some years more.

Eighty dollars buys a fancy meal.
Eighty dollars for a new outfit could be a steal.
Eighty purchases make a worthwhile garage sale.
Eighty envelopes are too much mail.

Eighty trips are a lot of travel time.
Eighty different restaurants are the way to dine.
Eighty days are almost a quarter of the year.
Eighty proof is not-a-strong beer.

Eighty-proof Vodka, however, makes your perfect drink.
Eighty glasses and you'll need the kitchen sink.
Eighty fish caught would be an overwhelming day.
Eighty friends and family sending wishes to say
Eighty different, *Hope you have a great birthday.*

Happy eightieth birthday.
Tom P., March 5, 2015

Karing Karyl

What? Spring Break, no place to rent!
Jeff and Karyl, on Heritage Oaks, were bent.
Ron and Jeff, golfing buddies, Naperville White Eagle Club.
Karyl and Linda were talking buddies, for our families, the hub.
Memories of Waubonsie High School days
Where Karyl taught, met our daughters that way.
We took their advice, rented a villa, in Florida on Samoset.
By month's end we were proud owners, you bet.

We loved every thing about our new place in the Sarasota sun.
Who would have guessed, the Potters and Grecues now having fun.
Dinners at Cafe Barbosa, delicious Italian cuisine.
Special occasions, friends gathered, always the scene.
Sharing life's ups and downs,
Karyl always positive, no frowns.
Energetic, fun as can be.
Kind and helpful to everybody.

Taking care of aging parents.
Visits, parties, much time spent.
Encouraged me many times
Through fearful tears, husband's health issue binds.
Inspiring to see her in the latest fashions.
Friends together taking workout classes.
During the COVID-19 quarantine,
Karyl, striped wallpaper, decorating queen.
Walking each day with Mary Kate,
Vacation trips with her mate.

Club home inherited from her Mother.
Fire pit added to lanai, and for guests, an afghan cover.
Modern updates, colorful added accessories.
Blue Jeans sofa replaced in Mother's memory.
Helped me start my *House Watch Service*.
You can do it. Don't be nervous.
To Karyl, my special friend, happy sixty-first birthday.
Glad we have fond memories along the way.
Karyl, November 7, 2020

Transformation

My sister's husband, Josh, is seventy years old.
The changes he has made in himself are a wonder to behold.

Sorry I missed your January birthday.
Distracted we were with my sister's health ways.

The twists and turns of life,
That come with thirty-six years as husband and wife.

Choices made, is life always fair?
Consequences play out, do we dare?

Life brings ups and downs.
Days bring smiles and frowns.

Souls search for truth and peace.
Love brings salvation and release.

A full life of friends and family,
Memories made for all to see.

Career and job changes, moving to Dallas,
The Texas Two Step, and The Yellow Rose of Texas.

Holidays and special events shared.
Always there for others for whom you cared.

Blessings of home, wife, church, career,
Blessings of the heart you hold dear.

Blessings of ministry to others,
Life story to share for sisters and brothers.

Beliefs, faith, spirit, soul,
Change, mature, deepen, grow.

Preparing for us unaware
For times in our future to bear.

The unforeseen, not expecting,
Parkinson's strikes your wife, unrelenting.

The ugly monster rears its head.
No one seems safe, even in bed.

Doctors, therapy, new medications.
For a time there are positive situations.

The years tick quickly by.
Suddenly we ask how and why?

Intervention, supervision, Memory Care Facility,
Loving, caring, redirecting of his beloved Ms. Connie.

And for the first time in many years,
Josh is free to be his old self again,
Without the fear and pain.

Knowing his wife is beautifully cared for,
He can now embrace what his life has in store.

So many changes already taking place.
Thank you God for direction and grace.

Welcome back to laughter and positivity,
Passion, health, and high energy.

Happy belated birthday.
Have fun, celebrate, is what I say.
Josh, June, 2020

When Jack Becomes Goose

J ack, you are Ron's golfing ears,
    As Ron has trouble his friends to hear.
A nd Ron, your eyes (Jack cannot see)
    Needed to find where Jack's golf ball will be.
C elebrating your seventy-third birthday,
    You will probably golf, your special way.
K indred golfing spirits Jack and Harry,
    When they partner with Ron and Kerry,
    Harry becomes Maverick, Jack becomes Goose.
    All four trying to win the hole and stay loose.

M ovie Group fun, each week a new flick.
    Always exciting to see what we pick.
    Who will score points or get blamed for the choice?
    We all chime in expressing our voice.
O ver-the-top, vacation journeys.
    You really love to travel, that's the key.
    Family, friends or exotic places to visit.
    With you and Char there is no limit.
R etired, Executive Director of the American Bowling Congress
    Years of countless service, or madness or famous greatness.
D ining out for special occasions,
    Your Char always knows the best locations.
I nvesting time in growing pineapple plants.
    Sharing with friends your offspring transplants.
N ewsworthy sports attract your attention.
    Bowling, golfing, your grandson's wrestling matches won.

I nvolved with Heritage Oaks Golf and Country Club
 Volunteering to help make it a better hub.
 Past Board member, Greens Committee now
 Thank you, Jack, for all you bring to our friendships. Wow.
  Happy seventy-third birthday
   Jack, July 2, 2020

Harry is a retired Navy pilot, thus the nicknames from *Top Gun*, Maverick and *Goose*.

A Friend Indeed

Kerry is definitely a friend indeed!
When we need help he is there with quick speed.
A Mac Book Air computer lesson needed by me.
Kerry came right over, home schooled me for free.

How do I arrange my poems in order, one, two, three,
For the chapters in my poetry book, you see?
He made it simple, made me practice, so I could be
Successful and excited, doing it right, his guarantee.

A burned-out lightbulb in the patio ceiling by our pool,
Kerry helped remove and replace the bulb. He had the right tool.
When Ron wanted more garage storage,
Kerry helped put up shelves. He had the knowledge.

He surprised us both with sturdy floats for the pool
So we could float around, relaxing, staying cool.
Whenever he and Annie come for dinner,
He brings Klondike bars, an ice cream winner.

Golfing partners, Ron and Kerry
Can be seen competing with Jack and Harry.
Can you believe Kerry had never seen the movie *Top Gun*,
So he did not understand the nicknames chosen for each one.

Harry, retired from flying for the navy, is of course Maverick.
Jack, his partner or wingman, Goose, of course his pick.
Kerry and Ron love beating Jack and Harry.
Every time they win, it makes their day merry.

We love having Kerry and Annie here in Sarasota.
Will truly miss both when you return to Minnesota.
So we are wishing you an early happy birthday
As we will not be with you in August to say,

Hope your special day
Is extra special in every way.
Kerry, August 3, 2020

Fun and Smiles

July is a busy month for Debbie and John
As both celebrate birthdays, another year to embark on.
2020, occurring the same week, their special day,
Sunday, the nineteenth, is John's birthday.
Debbie's, the twenty-fifth, is on Saturday.

When they moved to Heritage Oaks, the HO,
The Carolina Shrimp Boat had arrived, we would soon know.
They generously shared that shrimp with many.
Lavish dinner parties where there was plenty.
Carolina Cajun Cuisine at its best.
By this *cooking couple*, we were all blessed.

Fourth of July parties delicious and fun.
Grilling burgers and hot dogs with toasty buns.
Games to play for entertainment from the deck.
Ring toss around the pink Flamingo's neck.

Venice theater plays enjoyed by all.
Delicious dinner reservations before curtain call.
Your villa, tastefully decorated and always inviting.
Beautiful new pool, lush flowers, plants, delighting.

John, you're a good golfer, when making your putt
You have a wry smile and feel confident in your gut.
Debbie, when you golf, you have fun on that day
With friends close by, wearing aqua, you are happy anyway.

We see you both walking, out and about.
Always a smile and wave, catching up with a *shout out*.

Helping others is what you do.
You've been excellent friends to so many, too.
From all of us to both of you
Hope your birthdays are extra special, too.
John, July 19, 2020 Debbie, July, 25, 2020

Christmas Cantata was Joel Raney's, *Have You Heard*. At the choir party, before each poem stanza was read, a line from a different anthem was sung.

Church and Bible Study Threads

Create my Tapestry

Church threads, my first priority,
For a spiritually healthy family.
Relocating often to support my husband's career.
Finding a fitting church family to hold dear.
Bible studies to bring hope, not fear.
Calvary, Majesty, totally Heavenly,
Holy Story, Godly, Victory, Glory.

Genesis

1. God created the world in seven days.
2. Adam and Eve banished from Eden's Garden,
3. Because of sinful ways.
4. Cain kills Abel, then Seth born, another son.
5. From Seth to Noah, ten generations.

6. Noah builds an Ark,
   From Cypress bark.
7. Rain, Rain, Flood. As the waters did flow.
8. Rain, Rain, Rain, RAINBOW.

9. Shem, Japheth, and Ham are Noah's sons.
10. His descendants create thirteen nations.
11. Tower of Babel, nine generations to Abraham from Shem.
12. God promises a Nation, blessings, children to Father Abraham.

13. Abram goes to Canaan, Lot to Jordan.
14. Lot rescued by Abram's righteous hand.
15. God promises Abram and Sarai a son.
16. But Maid Hagar marries Abram, Ishmael becomes the one.

17. Abraham and Sarah, given a new name.
18. God promises Isaac, laughter, how insane!
19. Sodom and Gomorrah destroyed because of righteousness neglect.
20. Abraham lies and says, Sarah's my sister, to King Abimelech.

21. Isaac is born, Hagar and Ishmael sent away.
22. Isaac offered as sacrifice to see if Abraham's faith would stay.

23. Sarah dies and is buried at Hebron in Canaan, The Promised Land.
24. Isaac marries Rebekah as provided by God's hand.

25. Abraham dies, twins Esau and Jacob are born and bring new life.
26. Isaac, like his father, lies to King, about his wife.
27. Isaac tricked into blessing Jacob, instead of Esau, for more life strife.
28. Esau marries Ishmael's daughter and Jacob has his ladder dream.
29. Jacob is tricked into marriage to Leah. He works seven more years to marry Rachael. What a scheme.

30. Jacob has many sons, eventually twelve by four women.
31. Finally, Jacob moves away from father-in-law Laban.
32. Jacob wants to reconcile with Esau, his estranged brother, amid fears.
33. Jacob and Esau reconcile after many years.

34. Dinah, Jacob's daughter, in trouble with Prince Shechem.
35. Jacob's wife Rachael, and father Issac, both die and are buried in Bethlehem.
36. Esau's linage in this chapter is told.
37. Jacob's favorite son, Joseph, interprets dreams. He is given colorful coat, into slavery is sold.
38. He sells his brother and fails to keep promise to Tamar. How could Judah be so bold?

39. Joseph falsely accused and thrown in jail.
40. The Baker is killed and the Cupbearer makes bail,
41. Joseph's dream interpretation earns him a pass to Pharaoh's Palace, amazing place.
42. Brothers come for grain but don't recognize Joseph's face.

43. Second trip to Egypt, eleven brothers surprisingly treated royally.
44. But Joseph hides a silver cup in grain bag as one more testimony.
45. Joseph finally reveals his true identity.
46. All is forgiven with return Egypt trip for entire family!

47. Goshen is the pasture land given to Israelites.
48. Before Jacob dies, he blesses Joseph's sons
    Manasseh and Ephraim with all his might.
49. Then he blesses all twelve sons (twelve tribes of Israel),
    Judah's linage being David the King.
50. After Jacob's death, Joseph reassures his brothers, saying,
    God will deliver them, and to the Promised Land, will bring.

Major characters and chapters in which they are found:

Adam 4   Noah 10   Abraham 23   Issac 27

Esau 28, 36   Jacob 29–35   Joseph 50

Written as a summary of the book of Genesis for my
Bible Study Fellowship class
March, 2013

Eat Your Veggies, Too

❧

(based on the Bible Book of Daniel)

The Book of Daniel, culture and time it will transcend.
Is it really about the Fiery Furnace and the Lion's Den?
God's chosen people surrounded in Babylon captivity,
By Nebuchadnezzar's oppression and sin everywhere you could see.

A transforming training, men chosen of high quality.
Who would best survive, who would that be?
Daniel was determined not to be defiled,
But be faithful to God's rules, despite being riled.

He made a conscious decision as a teen
To be faithful to God, no matter the scene.
Instead of eating the King's rich food and wine,
Daniel and friends chose water and veggies on which to dine.

After ten days, Daniel and friends looked
better than all other trainees.
God's favor was on Daniel, daily in prayer on his knees.
The King found all four young men, ten times better than
All the magicians in his entire kingdom and land.

He gave them powerful positions of respect and trust
And relied on Daniel's Dream interpretation that was true and just.
King Nebuchadnezzar had a ninety-feet-
high, nine-feet-wide, golden idol made.
He did not want his fame to fade.

Everyone was to worship it each day.
But Daniel, and his three friends, refused to obey
Saying, *Our God can deliver us from any punishment*
But if He doesn't, doing what is right is still worth it.

So into a fiery furnace were thrown,
Shadrach, Meshach, and Abednego.
But God's Angel saved them, now the King would know
No other God saves like the God of
Shadrach, Meshach, and Abednego.
And God would continue to save Daniel and friends from every foe.

God was with them. He is with me and you.
All the times we find ourselves in the fiery furnace too.
God is not an insurance policy, vending machine, or lucky charm.
It is God's grace and love that saves us from harm.

When under pressure, always do what is right.
Not what the world would love in its sight.
Daniel remained faithful to God and God worked in his life.
At age eighty, there would be more strife.

Daniel worked under three kings: Nebuchadnezzar,
Belshazzar, and Darius.
Although he had a high position of respect and trust,
Jealousy would cause Daniel to be the aim of an attack.
Corrupt men had King Darius write a decree
that could not be taken back.

Anyone not praying to the King's idol, shall
be thrown into the lion's den.
When Daniel was found praying, the King
was informed by the jealous men.
Daniel said, *I chose my God. Prayer has always worked for me.*
I will not compromise, can't you see.

The King was distressed, even tried to save Daniel, too.
He said to Daniel, *May your God whom you*
serve continually, rescue you.
So Daniel was thrown into the Lion's Den, sealed with a stone.
The King could not sleep, eat, be entertained, or sit on his throne.

At first light of dawn, the King hurried to the den and found
Angels and prayer shut the lion's mouths,
kept Daniel alive and sound.
So King Darius did decree that day,
All people must revere the Saving God of
Daniel, who kept lions at bay.

So when you are in a fiery furnace or lion's
den, remember what to do:
Pray, do what is right, cling to God, and eat your veggies, too.

Written after a church sermon series on the Book of Daniel.
2019

Choices

So Lord, do the choices I make really bother
you, like *Hosea* says they do?
Does it really bother you what I say to the stranger I meet today?
Does it matter how my time is spent, my
money lent, my children bent?

Yes. It does matter and you made that quite clear
By giving me the *Minor Prophets* to study this year.
I already knew *David* was a man after *God's* heart.
I learned with a *Psalm* every day I should start.
Ester, working behind the scenes accomplishing *God's* will,
You will use me, if I pray daily, listen, take time to be still.
I'll hear and know what *God* has to say to me,
His Holy Spirit will guide me into what He wants me to be.
Remember *Jonah,* circumstances seemed so right?
I should be careful to stay in *God's* word so I don't lose sight.
God is patient with me. That's what it said in *Nahum's* book.
Am I patient with myself and others? I'll take a closer look.
Joel taught me a new meaning for the word fast.
*Give up things, so you'll have time for a
relationship with God that lasts.*
Habakkuk said, *when I become burned out or overbooked,
God is my sufficiency, to Him I must look.*
From *Micah* I learned, *God* will forgive
And post a *No Fishing* sign, that's how I must live.
Because *God* helps me forgive and forget,
Only then do I experience freedom from my sin and debt.
I knew end times would someday come.
I didn't think about that, I didn't want to be glum.

Zechariah helped make it so very clear.
The rapture, the Second Coming, could all be so near.

Yes, Lord, the choices really do bother you, like *Hosea* says they do.
It really bothers you what I say to the stranger I meet today.
It matters how my time is spent, my money lent, my children bent.
Yes, the choices I make do matter and you made that quite clear,
By giving me the *Minor Prophets* to study this year.

Written as a summary of The Minor Prophets
Bible Study Fellowship
1986-1987

Class Commitment

This past year I've loved each of you in a special way,
And will cherish your excitement and
willingness to share each Tuesday.

Your commitment to excellence and completed lessons,
The special sharing that occurred at luncheons,
Each answered prayer request,
The way you always gave your best,
Your love and concern and support for each other,
You definitely were like a special mother.

The verse that was on your name tag this year,
I pray you'll always keep in your heart most dear.
It is better to get wisdom than gold,
As in *Proverbs 16:16* we are told.
*And to get understanding is to be
Chosen above silver* by you and me.

So read your Bible each summer day.
Pray that God will guide and keep you in His way.
The Lord is faithful. That we know.
He loves and cares about us so.
Just as He cared for Israel, His chosen race,
He cares about each one, no matter what
the circumstance, time, or place.

Don't forget *Psalm 103.*
It has a special meaning to me.
*The Lord is gracious and compassionate. To anger He is slow,
And abounding in loving kindness.* That we know.

His Holy Spirit will help you be
Producers of the Fruits of the Spirit, *Galatians 5:23.*
Love, joy, self-control, kindness, gentleness,
Peace, patience, goodness, and faithfulness.

I'm grateful for the opportunity to be your leader this year
I pray God will bless you and hold you in His palm most dear.

Bible Study Fellowship Class
The Minor Prophets, 1986–1987

Matthew

Tears were shed when I left that day.
They usually are when I head a new way.

All the friends left behind.
Four years of memories in my mind.
Leaving California sunshine and warm days .
Moving to the Midwest had my two teenage daughters in dismay.

God's proven faithfulness and providence in my heart,
As my family and I looked forward to a new start.
Naperville was windy, flat, and cold.
I prayed, *Please, Lord, help me be bold.*

We each faced different trials that were hard to bear,
Which allowed us to see God's Power answer each prayer.
So many churches from which to choose,
A friend found, I didn't want to lose.

School Counselor from Bible Study Fellowship past.
Strong relationship with Jen and Jill to last.
Godly advice when badly needed.
Loving words that were heeded.

Bible Study Fellowship close to our home.
New friends in Christ, no longer alone.
Substitute Discussion Leader, my part.
You know how that warmed my heart.

The Book of Matthew taught me day by day,
Let go, Linda. Let God have His way.
The Bible is my Survival Manual,
Today and in end times prophesied by Daniel.

My King is coming, I know not when.
I'll extravagantly serve like Mary until then.
When Jesus faced the agony of the Cross,
His energies focused on loving others, instead of being boss.

Composure, compassion, conviction, the example He set.
These in me He intends to be met.
God, You are the Potter, I am the clay.
My first response to crisis won't be to panic, but pray.

Help me not rely on a feeling,
Claim your promises, expect a miracle of healing.
What a great cost Jesus was willing to pay
For my forgiveness and salvation today.

I am not worthy, but of great worth.
I am so special because of new birth.
It is finished. Paid in full.
Bold access, eternal life, free to love, my sins made null.

Jesus's Resurrection, magnificent to me.
I am the glove, God is the hand empowering me to be.
The Fruit of the Spirit for the world to see
So all will bring honor and glory to God for all eternity.

Come and see the empty tomb. He is risen. Go and tell.
Disciple and missionary the world. Make it spiritually well.
Lo I am with you always to the close of the ages.
Treasure and obey what Matthew wrote in the Bible pages.

Bible Study Fellowship
I began the study of Matthew in California, September, 1988.
I completed the study of Matthew in Naperville, Illinois, 1989.

Share

Acts 1 and 2

Jesus taught everyone who believed and
followed him, in three short years.
Then Jesus was crucified on a cross and
his followers shed lots of tears.
But He came back to life, before going to
heaven, said to his followers,
Now you have the big job of becoming teachers.
Whatever I taught while I was alive on earth each day,
Now it's up to you to remember just what I did say.

At first it seemed an impossible task,
The disciples prayed and for help they did ask.
God did not leave them alone. He sent a
helper called the Holy Ghost,
Who would strengthen them and their
hearts to help God the most.
Those early Christians depended on support from each other every day
To know how to live, work, treat others, and play.

Not everyone believed in God, so life was not easy.
The Christians did everything together to keep life breezy.
They worshipped, ate, and praised God together,
Devoted themselves to teaching, fellowshipping, and sharing forever.

They knew God's word is for everyone, so each day
The Christians would look for words they could say
That might make a difference in someone's life,
Causing that person to become a Christian, giving up his strife.

Many believed because those Christians
shared what Jesus had to say.
The church grew and grew and GREW each day.

God's Word is for everyone. That is true.
Now the challenge of sharing Jesus is up to me and you.
Go home and trust that Jesus will give you the words to say
So you can share what you learned here at Bible School each day
With someone who does not know about Jesus and his love.
Know I'll be praying for each of you to God above.

This rhyming story was written for elementary-age children
attending Vacation Church School. Being a teacher, I
believe rhyming makes learning more fun. June, 2011

"I Can Walk"

Acts 3 and 4

The man in our story today, was crippled and could not walk.
A friend or family member would come to
his house each day to talk,
And carry the crippled man to the Temple Gate to beg,
Hoping to get money, since the man could
not work because of his leg.

The crippled man liked to sit in the shade of the Beautiful Gate,
Crying, *Money for this poor man, because of my legs I have to wait.*
Day after day he would hold out a small cup,
Hoping for money donations to fill the cup up.

One day, the crippled man asked Peter
and John for coins for his cup.
Peter smiled at the man as he lifted his face up.
Peter looked right into that man's eyes and said,
I don't have any money for you, but I'll give you what I have instead.

You see, Peter and John were disciples of Jesus that day,
And they knew that Jesus could heal if they would just pray.
So Peter said, *In the name of Jesus Christ, get up and walk!*
The man, who'd been crippled since birth,
walked, jumped, and talked.

He talked, praised God, and believed that day,
And was a powerful witness to all that Peter and John would say.

Peter took the opportunity to share the message of God with all,
He told about Jesus's life, death, and
resurrection to large and small.

The temple guard and Sadducees didn't like what Peter had to say.
You guessed it. They put Peter and John
back in prison that same day.
Most people were good listeners and
believed what Peter had to say.
Thousands had their lives changed and became Christians that day.

God's Word is life changing. That is so true.
God's Word is life changing for me and for you.

This rhyming story was written for elementary-age children
attending Vacation Church School. Being a teacher I
believe rhyming makes learning more fun. June, 2011

Comfort and Anchor in Terrible Troubles

Acts 9

We meet a new person in the Bible today,
Who did not know Jesus or even how to pray.
His name was Saul and he made choices that were bad,
But then he believed in Jesus and that made God glad.

He changed his name to Paul and had so much to say.
He went many places teaching people about Jesus every day.
Paul was preaching in the city of Jerusalem one night,
Trying to help men understand Jesus with all his might.

But the men would not believe and told lies about Paul.
The angry men started a fight, soon there had to be a police call.
The men told more lies and guess what happened to Paul?
He was thrown into jail and handcuffed to the wall.

Paul had more troubles, illness, hunger, pain,
A terrible storm with lots of thunder, lightning, and rain.
It rained so hard, the waves were so high,
The wind so strong, the waves almost touched the sky.

His ship hit a big rock, it was late at night.
Paul prayed to God until morning light.
He gave comfort and hope to all those on his boat.
Encouraged them to have faith that God would keep them afloat.

Paul shared God's love with everyone he knew.
Taught people God's Word would always comfort them, too.
So remember, no matter how terrible things might be,
God will always comfort and be an anchor for you and me.

Set Free

Acts 12

Peter was arrested and thrown in jail.

He was jailed for being a Christian. There was no bail.

Four guards and two heavy chains. He was ready for death.

It would take a miracle to save him as he took his last breath.

Surprise! An angel appeared to Peter in his cell.

And said, *Quick! Get up! You're going to be saved.* Well—

As those two heavy chains fell to the ground,

Peter left the jail cell. He was no longer bound.

Peter thought he was having a dream,

But the angel said, *This is real. Do not scream!*

Astonished, Peter ran to Mary's house, friends there to pray.

They celebrated, God, set free Peter, that very day!

232

Surprises From Heaven

Acts 27 and 28

Remember the story about a man named Saul,
Who started believing in Jesus, changed his name to Paul.

Once he was in a terrible storm, shipwrecked at night.
Everyone aboard ship was in a terrible fright.

But God gave them comfort and a special piece of land
That was an island with a beach and sand.

The name of this island was Malta and meant,
A safe place, refuge for crew mates, tired and spent.

The island people welcomed the men and built a fire,
So everyone could get dry, warm, watch the flames go higher.

Paul gathered sticks and set them in the flames.
Suddenly everyone was calling his name.

One stick was actually a very poisonous snake called a viper.
When it bit Paul on his hand, it made him hyper.

Everyone thought Paul would die from the poisonous bite.
But God surprised everyone that night.

Paul did not die because God protected him that day.
So many islanders listened to everything Paul had to say.

Paul stayed in Malta for three months, praying each day,
Many island people were healed in a miraculous way.

Even a shipwreck couldn't keep Paul from sharing God's love
And showing how *God surprises us* from heaven above.

Titus

Titus is the name of a letter, the Apostle Paul wrote.
Paul's purpose was training, for a younger person, to promote.
Paul wrote, *All I have learned may be helpful to you*
In ministering to your church in Crete, too.

Paul lists ways to live to be pleasing to God each day
And why we should want to live that way.
Self-control, sound faith, love, kindness, and respect for all.
Teach what is good, be temperate, in marriage be faithful.

When Christ comes into your life and reveals His Grace,
You should act and be different in every place.
Turn from godless living and sinful pleasures,
Looking forward to your heavenly treasures.

Live in the evil world with wisdom, devotion to God,
And righteousness, because of your Salvation, each day you trod.
Obey the Laws of the land,
As long as they do not contradict God's hand.

Be gentle, speak no evil, and to all show courtesy.
Avoid quarreling, living for Christ is the way to be.
We have all been broken, slaves to pleasures and passions,
Hateful, jealous, envious, all the wrong things our decisions.

Thankfully *God in his Mercy and God in His Grace*
Has secured my Salvation with a heavenly place.

Written after a church sermon series on Titus.
October, 2019

Acts of Peter,
Acts of Paul

Powerful Gospel witness to all.
Beginning on Pentecost, with tongues of fire,
Each apostle was given evangelism desire.

Denying *Peter* transformed that day.
His power-filled message changed lives to a better way.
From Jerusalem to Asia, Greece, and Rome,
Paul willingly left security and home.

Missionary Journeys over land and sea,
Hardships and crises to encourage you and me.
The lessons I learned from *Paul*
Are in the Bible to benefit us all.

Acts 1: Instead of being anxious each day of my life,
I'll pray while waiting for God's timing, to work out my strife.
Acts 4–7: I'll pray, not for ease, but boldness and power.
I'm never alone. The Holy Spirit is with me each hour.

Acts 8–9: When God calls me to new tasks,
He equips me so I can do what He asks.
The bigger the job God has for me,
The more time I need to spend with him on my knees.

Acts 9–11: Trials are opportunities to explore my comfort zone,
For expansion and growth, still I'm never alone.
I know I can say, *Lord, things are tough. I'm not sure what to do.*
I thank God that I have you.

You're the only one who can help anyway.
I'm expecting to see your Power at work,
your blessings unfold today.

Thessalonians: Father, I even thank you for the trials today,
That teach me patience as I pray.
Endurance, comfort, hope, all come from you,
Trust, faith, perseverance, and peace, too.

Corinthians: A constant encourager, I want to be
To my friends, strangers, and family.
This is one way to witness God's love for me,
As I encourage all I see.

Galatians: When I died on the cross with Jesus,
two selves now struggle within,
The new life by the Spirit, the old by flesh and sin.

The Rhythm of Romans I'll never forget.
Sin, salvation, sanctification, setting self aside, service, you bet.
I is in the center of sin. Take heed.
It easily happens when I think of only my need.

Justification, Just for me.
Just as if I'd never sinned—I'm free.
Free from slave's bondage, sin, and shame.
Freed by the blood of Jesus slain.

God's grace gift, all I do is believe.
His righteousness I then receive,
And the sanctification process begins for me.
A lifetime of learning what God wants me to be.

For whatever was written in earlier ages,
Was written for our instruction at different stages.
That through encouragement of the scripture and perseverance,
We might have hope in every circumstance. *Romans 15:4*

Written as a summary for my students after studying
The Life and Letters of Paul
Bible Study Fellowship
1987-1988

Do I Have an Idol?

Well, let me see. What in the world could it be?
First Commandment A place for everything, everything in its place.
That is a challenge I can embrace.
Second Commandment Vacuuming and dusting make me feel fine.
Third Commandment Make it sparkle, make it shine.
Why is this job always mine?
Fourth Commandment Keep dirty hands off every clean door.
Keeping the house clean is an endless chore.

Fifth Commandment Cleaning includes raking yard leaves and sticks.
Sixth Commandment, Yard work must be
done every week unless one is sick.
Seventh Commandment Always keep your house straight,
That's the best way to impress your mate.
Eighth Commandment Clean every Friday,
regardless of sunshine or rain.
Cleaning is never done. Always time to start again.
Ninth Commandment Isn't cleanliness the best way to heaven?
Tenth Commandment Clean for six days. Rest on day seven.

Why do I go to church? I won't hedge.
At church, they always talk about my *Pledge*.

Softball, tennis, I love it all.
As long as it includes a ball.
Racquetball, handball, They're all the same.
I have the racquet. Just name the game.
Basketball, golf, do I have a taker?
What a way to give praise to my maker.

Soccer, baseball, even bowling,
I love to keep those balls rolling.
Do I have an idol? Well let me see.
That would never have occurred to me.
You say ball is my whole life,
Interferes with my children and wife?

No way! Couldn't happen to me.
Do I have an idol? Well let me see.

Who me, have an idol? Well can't you see,
I'm too busy to decide what that would be.
Got my towel and swimming gear.
Certainly hope there's a swimming pool here.
Backstroke, sidestroke, Australian crawl,
Breaststroke, butterfly, I know them all.

I love to dive off the diving board too,
There isn't any dive I can't do.
Back dive, front flip, even a jackknife.
That's my favorite thing to do in life.

I'm ready for a swim most any day.
I love it! What more can I say?

Written for a skit at the Westlake Lutheran Church family retreat.
Mother, Father, Daughter, 1986

Easter

Glory and honor are due your name.
For every day, Jesus, you are the same.

Risen now as you were risen then.
Each day to rise in our hearts again.

We serve you with love and joy.
As we teach each girl and boy.

What a privilege to be
Teachers of, *God's love is free!*

God's love is for you.
God's love is for me.

Farewell, Westlake Church Family,

God's providence never left the Potters in a lurch.
The Kubics' home came with orthodontist, piano teacher, church.
Westlake Lutheran's been a special church family.
We'll always cherish each eventful memory.

Personal, meaningful worship in fresh new ways,
Exciting Sunday School lessons and Come Together Sundays.
Macrame fish nets, eating Scripture Cake,
Advent projects, Easter crosses to make.

Measuring Noah's Ark in the church parking lot,
Planning lessons to interest both teen and tot.
Flash light candles for Christmas Eve night,
Jennifer and Jill serving as acolytes.

Sounds of children's voices from the Junior Choir,
Anthems and Bell Choir music to inspire.
Confirmation of Jennifer and classes for Jill,
Learning about the Lutheran Church, Bible, and God's will.

Youth Group adventures, Yolijwa fun,
Hands Across America in the California sun.
Delicious but crazy Chili McGoo,
Hunger walks to help feed the world, too.

Nursery service with a smile,
Watching Bride Sonja float down the aisle.
Challenges of Council, special seaside retreat,
Rewards of Every Member Commitment to meet.

Craft Fair with Advent ornaments, baked goodies to share,
Encouraging words, friendly faces everywhere.
Lutheran Church Women and my Secret Pal,
Love and support from every gal.

Christmas caroling in the chilly night air,
At Vons, for Jenny, spreading cheer everywhere.
Lenten Prayer Partners and devotions to write,
Easter Morning Service with Resurrection Light!

Strength felt from Prayer Chain Power,
Knowing our church family was there each hour.
Joys to share, hearts to mend,
Love and acceptance of each special friend.

It's truly been a privilege to be a part
Of each life, to serve from the heart.
And so it is with love we send,
Thank you, farewell, until we meet again.

If you ever long for wind and snow,
Just come visit the Potters in Chicago.
February 1, 1989

Yes, We Appreciate You

In honor of *Teacher Appreciation Sunday,* the children
have a song to sing to the tune of, *Jesus Loves Me.*

Teachers love us, this we know.
For you're always showing us so.
Today we thank you and we pray.
God will keep you in His way.

Chorus: Yes, we appreciate you. (point to teacher)
Yes, we appreciate you. (point to teacher)
Yes, we appreciate you. (point to teacher)
And all you say and do!

Teachers teach us of God's love,
That He sends us from above,
And how He cares for me each day,
Guiding and protecting what I do and say.

Chorus: (same as above)

In case you haven't figured it out,
Teacher Appreciation is what it's about.
We thank you for teaching us this year about being:
Listening Disciples (Holds up card, reads out loud)
Believing Followers (same)
Caring Servants (same)
Faithful Witnesses (same)
Joyful People at Worship (same)

Chorus: (same as above)

Yes, we appreciate you!

We know it's not easy being a *Teacher*, since our Sunday
School starts early Sunday morning. This song is in
honor of that fact. No disrespect intended by putting
our words to a familiar tune, *Low in the Grave He Lay*.

Tired in her bed she lay,
From working night and day.
Warm in her covers she wanted to stay,
My Sunday School Teacher on Sunday.

But Up from her bed she arose,
For there's something important that she knows.
She knows God loves her and she wants to share,
With Sunday School children everywhere.
She arose,
She arose,
From her warm bed she arose.

Teachers are many things to different people:

T trustworthy, tender, thankful, true, teaching
E earnest, eager to serve, encouraging
A adoring of God, able, alert, amazing, accepting, abiding
C cheerful, considerate, creative, charitable, caring
H helpful, honest, humble, happy, hopeful, God honoring
E ever ready, effective, engaging, exciting
R ready, reverent, radiant, redeemed, respected, rejoicing
S servant, special, saint, saved, shepherd, supporting

We thank you teachers for showing us the light.
Living for Jesus is the only way that's right.

Moaning Boy Cured Skit

Moaning Boy (Boy moans, holds stomach, head, throat, arms, legs).

Mother (Mother comes in, looks at boy, makes a quizzical expression with hands and face, feels his head, takes his pulse, leaves, comes back with food tray, shows it to audience, gives it to boy).

Narrator Food, yes, maybe food will help.

Lower your cholesterol, don't eat the fat.

Take away the sugar, you'll be a lean cat.

Let's hope some food will cure all his ills,

So we won't need a doctor, won't need the pills.

Moaning Boy (tries food, enjoys it, feels better, smiles, looks at audience, moans again, Mother takes food and leaves stage).

Knock, Knock.

Doctor (enters, examines boy, takes temperature, pulse, listens to heart, holds up pill bottle).

Narrator (talks while doctor examines the boy).

Doctor, doctor help this boy, please.

Does he have a cough, does he have a sneeze?

Make him feel better. Cure him quick.

We don't want to hear him moan.

We don't want to see him sick.

Doctor (leaves stage).

Moaning Boy (starts moaning again).

Knock, Knock

Music (Music enters, snapping fingers, dancing).

Moaning Boy	(starts listening to music, feels better, snaps fingers, dances).
Narrator	What's this? Music, yes, music will help.
	Hum a tune, sing a song.
	Play that jam box all day long.
	Music, music soothes the soul.
	Music, music, that's my goal.
Music	(leaves stage).
Moaning Boy	(starts moaning again).
Knock, Knock	
Exercise	(Exercise enters, does jumping jacks).
Moaning Boy	(gets up and exercises).
Narrator	Music, food, doctor, haven't helped. Maybe exercises will.
	Jog, walk, run or bike,
	Swim, surf, take a hike,
	Stretch those muscles, don't just sit.
	Get up and exercise and you'll feel fit.
Exercise	(leaves stage).
Moaning Boy	(starts moaning again).
Knock, Knock	
Narrator	We've tried every measure.
	We've tried everything.
	What possible solution
	Could this next person bring?
Sunday School Teacher	(enters and sits beside boy, holds up Bible, and begins reading Bible stories).
Narrator	I think this boy is better, he's no longer ill.
	We won't need a doctor, we won't need a pill.
	He's finally found the reason, that his heart wants to sing.

It's the message of Jesus's Love that the Sunday
School teacher brings.

So we want to thank you teachers,
For showing us children the light,
That Jesus is the only thing,
That can make us feel right.

So if you don't come to Sunday School,
You'll grow up to be sad.
You'll never know just what you missed,
And someday wish you had.
So come and join us every week,
For fellowship and fun,
For Bible study, singing, crafts, and prayer,
There's something for everyone.

Confirmation

God made you in his own special way.
He loves you each and every day.

God gave you life as his unique gift.
Our praises to him we daily lift.

You are special! That is very true.
There's nothing with God's help you can't do.

God will give you peace and comfort, too,
His power to do God's work in you.

So on this your Confirmation Day,
May you remember as you pray,

Depend on God in every way,
In everything you do and say.

May God always be your best friend.
May you love and serve him to the end.

Why, God?

Ellen and I, tennis partners for several years.
John and Ellen unable to have children, sadness, fears.
Was there another option?
Ten years of waiting, finally *adoption*.

The prayers that seemed to have been answered, *no,*
Were finally answered, yes, and so . . .
A baby boy. Now a happy family.
Mommy, daddy, baby made three.

We moved from Indianapolis to California.
Two years later, January 28, 1986, historic day.
Bible Study Fellowship at church that morning.
Space Shuttle explosion we were told before leaving.

No amount of Bible study could answer *why?*
A fatal Space program disaster, I would have to try
Explain to my daughter who wrote a letter
To Christa McAuliffe, the first-in-space teacher.

I could not go home, needed time to think and pray.
How God, will I ever explain this day?
My favorite beach spot, sound of waves, smell of spray,
Tide comes in, goes out, come what may.

I knew God answered prayers in my life.
Sent me a husband, safely returned him from Vietnam strife.
Gave us children, healed cancer, provided homes in a safe place.
Why this teacher who stimulated interest in space?

Had notebooks full of prayer requests, their answers recorded.
My tears of anguish, pain over an event so sordid.

Upon returning home, a phone call, a voice from my past.
My friend Ellen, Why had she called at last?
Did not feel like talking, just wanted to be alone.
But there was something in her voice, her tone.

Are you sitting down, I have overwhelmingly great news.
Just saw my doctor. After all these years, God still pursues.
I am going to have a baby, a miracle indeed.
I phoned to share my news, get you up to speed.

God creates, He doesn't puppet control
Human choices that take their toll.
Just as I cannot explain why Ellen is now having a baby
I cannot explain why the shuttle exploded, lack of knowledge maybe.

We may never know the answer to our WHY whine
But we do know God continues to create,
answer prayers in HIS TIME.

Stewardship

Dr. Terri Paulson called yesterday.
I thought he called to just say, Hey.
He asked, *Will you give a talk in church on serving the Lord each day,*
And how you accomplish this in your own way?

I said, *Sure, I know just the story I want to tell*
The *Funster Family* went on vacation and well,
Had so much fun, they decided to stay
Just one more week, just one more day.
Stayed away, having fun, in the surf, in the sun.
They spent their life having such a ball,
Forgot what was important to all.
When they finally returned to Westlake,
Mom and Dad were shocked to see,
Where the church used to be,
Now there was a wide-open space,
A shopping center in its place!

The kids said, *Why are you so upset today?*
We were never there anyway.
Voice said, *God gave each talents in a different amount,*
Which are to be used. Someday you'll have to account.
Mother said, *He gave me so few. What am I to do?*
Dad said, *It takes money to run a church. What can I say?*
We never have enough money, even after payday.

Voice said, *Time's the one thing He's given to each an equal share.*
You can't complain God's been unfair.
Mother said, *Twenty-four hours He gave us to take.*
Why thirty-six hours of choices to make?

Voice said, *Ahh, that's where the rub comes in.*
Dad said, *I blame it on original sin.*

Voice said, *When the days of your life have quickly passed,*
Only what's done for God will last.
Dad said, *You make it sound like I'm going to my grave today,*
My life spent, wasted away.
Mother said, *How did my life become so*
busy, to the point I feel dizzy?

Have you been on vacation, gone too long,
From a life of dedication, joy and song?
Do you know *His Voice*, what he wants to say to you?
Do you pray daily, read the Bible, too?
It doesn't take money or talent, you see,
To find what *God* wants you to be.
He took Moses, Samuel, David, Paul, trained them day by day,
To follow Him, to work in HIs way.
You say, *Yes, I've been away.*
I want to start serving today.
I want to change. Where's the door?
I want to serve Him more."
Then:
Pray to God every day,
To use your time for God's way.
Listen for God to speak to you
Through the Bible, what to do.
Wait for God's guidance and light.
He gives wisdom and might.
Read the Bible, feed on God's word. He's the bread of life,
Always there in health and strife.
Say yes, when Pastor calls with a job for you.
Yes, what can I do?

Yes, I will take a leap in faith today.
Yes, I want the right way.
Yes, I want to at least try.
Yes, I will not sigh.
Yes, I want to see,
What God wants me to be.
He'll stretch time so His work gets done.
See you through if you're the one.
He'll give energy, ideas, words to say.
You'll know you're on the right way.
He'll replace that frown, that sadness.
Help you serve Him with gladness.
Galatians 2:20
I died with Jesus on the Cross.
It was my gain, not loss.
I, myself, no longer live.
Christ lives in me His power to give.
He gives power to me each day,
So I know how to live, what to say.
Serve God. You have to make that choice.
Serve God. You can be God's voice.
Serve God. It's not easy, it never is.
But you're only giving back time that's actually His.
Serve God. Serve his church today.
Serve God by what you do and say.
Baking, cleaning, evangelizing, fellowshipping, painting, praying,
Singing, teaching, tithing, typing, visiting, worshipping.

As for me and my house, we will serve the Lord (Joshua 24:15, KJV).
Serve the Lord with gladness (Psalm 100:2, KJV).
Through love, serve one another (Galatians 5:13, ESV).

October, 1986

253

Talk to God

Praise, thanksgiving, confession, petition, intercession.
  For some, these parts are needed for their expression.
  God watches over me, by faith, this I know.
  He loves me each day the same, no ebb or flow.

Relating to God in the moment, we talk to Him as a best Friend.
  Knowing that when all else fails, God will be there past the end.
  God forgives all my sins, covers me with His Grace.
  God gives peace, hope, and purpose in my life for all I face.

Ask, and it will be given to you. Seek and you will find.
  Knock and it will be opened to you. To all I remind.
  When I feel panic, anxiety, or fears.
  God has the answers, helps dry my tears.

You can talk to God anytime, any day.
  You can talk to God any place, any way.
  Father, You are good. I need help. They need help. Thank you.
  In Jesus's Name. Amen. Max Lucado's simple prayer so true.

Evolving, our life puzzle pieces to fit, or threads to weave,
  Trusting in God's power to answer prayer, we believe.
  God's ears are always listening when we grieve,
  He comforts and gives peace our panic to relieve.

Relationships take time to develop. That's what God desires.
  Honesty with God every day will help us acquire.
  The more we talk to God, the more we see our need
  To stay close, in contact, and feel God's saving Love indeed.

Transformed by Music

Our choir practice begins with prayer
For God's peace, hope, healing, loving care,
For our Music to Minister and Reach
Those who come to hear the Pastor preach.

Have you heard? Have you heard?

We sign out our music to keep track,
Making sure each anthem is returned to the rack.
Warm up with correctly formed vowel sounds,
So voices will collectively abound.

In a quiet stable in Bethlehem, under starlight glowing above.

We practice hard to perfect the score,
Hope our congregation will adore.
Altos, Sopranos, Tenors, and Basses,
Learning our parts so we don't sing in the wrong places.

Be aware of rests and beats per measure,
Stagger breathing or breathing together.
Watch for forte, pianissimo,
Crescendo and decrescendo.

Come, Emmanuel, Come, Emmanuel, Come!

Nicole Masterfully directs our choir,
Helping us achieve a note higher.
We love her solos any Sunday.
Her voice, angelic in every way.

Oh holy night, the stars are brightly shining.

While we sing, we must watch Nicole
So no one has an unexpected solo role.
To help us at home, she sends a sound link,
Practice our anthem, make us think.

The choir is more than a group that sings.
We are family and each person brings,
Support, love, caring ways,
Comforting words spoken for difficult days.

Peace to all, peace to all on Ear-TH!

Thank you, Nicole, for directing us.
Your patience, humor, and leadership
Keep us challenged, and help us get a grip
On transforming music on paper
To a message for all to savor.
And in the process, we've become
Transformed as well by what we've sung.

Have you heard? Christ is born! On Christmas Day in the morning.
December 2019

This poem was read at our choir Christmas party. We sang Joel
Raney's cantata, Have You Heard, for Christmas, so between each
poem stanza, a line from the anthems was sung.

Get Well Threads

Create my Tapestry

What can I do, what can I say,
To make you feel better today?
Maybe a poem will put a smile on your face
Until you are feeling better and back in the race.

Get Well Riddle

My twelve years old granddaughter had spine surgery to correct her scoliosis. To make home recovery fun, I gave her a gift and riddle each day.

While you are healing and resting in bed,
Hope food tastes better *in something red*.
Red plastic dishes

To track your progress along the way,
Make an entry every day.
Journal and four colored pens

Hope this brings a smile to your face
And *keeps you warm* as you pick up your pace.
Soft knitted head band

A new friend has come to keep you company,
But will *he melt* your heart before you count to three?
Snowman pin

People will say, *What a stud*, when they see you.
Hope you enjoy wearing them, *two.*
Fake diamond studs

As they go around your *wrist* today,
Each *spot* stands for love coming your way.
Ladybug bracelet

Get your *needles* ready to go,
When you are well, you'll have something to show.
Yarn for a scarf

Hope you are feeling more *stable*.
Please enjoy this *new label*
Horse stable sign for door

Thought it would be *fund*,
For your horse camp *day$* in the *$un*.
$$$ for horse camp

Here's something you can *play alone*,
While you spend some days at home.
Cards

We love you, and Jesus loves you, *two*.
Hold out your *wrist* and figure out the clue.
Two cross bracelets

These will keep you *warm* when you *ride*,
Or when it's *chilly* at your *bedside*.
Horse-pattern knee socks

Eat this when you're hungry and ready to dine.
Cheer for your *favorite team* at the same time.
Indiana University red/white pasta

This gift is *sketchy*, to say the least.
Try *drawing* a horse, instead of a beast.
Pens, pencils, sketch pad

Just because you are so *sweet*,
Here are *Kisses* to eat.
Hershey Kisses

Enjoy opening your gifts, Taylor. January 20, 2014
Her surgery was successful, and Taylor played high school volleyball
for four years and her track team placed 6th at the State Meet
her Junior year.

Grandson

Born on the fourth of July.
You were our firecracker guy.
Your Dad did a backward flip and said, *Wow.*
I finally have a son now.

That was so many years ago.
It's been great to watch you grow.
Thinking of our conversation at the pool,
In the shade trying to stay cool.

You asking me about my life here.
What kinds of things I like during the year.
You shared your workout times for basketball.
And games coming up, North vs. South and all.

Your kindness and appreciation will linger in my heart
As I think of you growing up so capable and smart.
We say a prayer for you each day.
Pappy and I are just a phone call away.

We understand life has given you a challenge or two.
We support you in whatever you need to do.
Whatever the course you need to take,
Whatever you need to do to make
Yourself feel better in do season,
Whatever the rhythm or reason.

You may even gain lessons in dealing with strife.
Lessons that will benefit you later in your life.

You may question why this season,
But someday look back and see the reason.
I know God has a plan for you.
And will strengthen you in all you do.

Counseling and medication helped my grandson for several
months, but would not be the final answer. 2020

Bum Knees Surgery

Pastor Jaime,
Playing softball is supposed to be fun
But sounds like you did not score a home run.

We were dismayed to hear what happened to you.
But very grateful for a successful surgery, too.

Cartilage, ligaments, tendons and all.
Bet your surgeon did not have a ball.

Challenging surgery to fix both messed-up knees
So you could be good as can be.

We're thankful everything went so well
And hope you are soon feeling swell.

We worry about your level of pain.
In your life you don't need more rain.

Take care of yourself, prayers coming your way.
May you feel new healing, each new day.

Uncertain times, hard to endure.
Of God's hope and healing we can be sure.

Many uncertainties about the quarantine
We pray you do not get COVID-19

May you feel God's protection and power
Every day and every hour.
March, 2020

Pastor Jaime had surgery, began rehab, and reached his goal of preaching Easter Sunday Sermon on April 12, 2020. Rehab continued for several months. June 15, 2020, he was able to walk with a walker. It would be September before he could walk unassisted.

Oh! No!

Oh! No! Ella, You injured your knee.
Can't play soccer or run in P.E.

Wearing a brace to help yourself heal.
We are sending you money, so here's the deal.

Thought you could *book it*, buy a new book to read,
Or *eat it*, maybe ice cream or yogurt is what you need.

Or *wear it*, buy a new outfit for fall,
Or *doll it*, buy an outfit for your doll. You make the call.

Get well soon. Feel better today.
Spend the $$$ in your special way.

When our granddaughter Ella injured her knee, she was
participating in a *Book It* contest at school, the more books
she read, the more points she earned. Wanting to write a fun
poem to make Ella smile and laugh, I was inspired by the *Book It*
theme. Sending money from a distance, seems to be a safe fit.
Fourth grade, 2013-2014

Prayer Shawl Healing

Father Tommy
Your Lord and Savior is Risen Indeed!
Always there to meet your every need.
We hope this prayer shawl helps you stay
Warm, cozy, and snug in every way.

Wrapped in love and prayers for what you're dealing
For strength, comfort, recovery, peace, and total healing.
As it wraps around your shoulders and arms,
Be reminded God heals you from all that harms.

You may wonder why me, how long, going where?
Rest assured God will *take* you there.
God will be with you every step of the way
During chemo, surgery, recovery, every day.

Wrap yourself in Ron's Prayer Shawl, get ready for the ride
Know many are praying and God will provide.

We fondly remember: Past conversations, our Italy trip with your
expert Vatican guide, male voices at Vespers, a delicious Italian dinner,
busy streets, cathedrals, and a roof top view of city.
Naperville family reunions, Punta Gouda gatherings, weddings, babies,
candles lit and prayers said for both families.
Christmas Eve TV service from the Vatican with your voice translating
to the world, and your parents presenting the gifts to the Pope
himself.
The good, the bad, the ugly, but always with love and grace, forgiveness
and peace, confidence for a better world where there is food for all—
both physical and spiritual.

In this Easter Season, this beginning of Holy Week, when we are reminded that the Lamb became the Light, I thank you for being that Light for me and many others. Get well soon.

Palm Sunday, April 14, 2019

Tom and Margaret Mary were our next-door neighbors for twenty-six years in Naperville, Illinois. Their oldest son, Tommy, was a priest at the Vatican, in Rome, Italy, for ten years. After returning to the States, Father Tommy was diagnosed with cancer.

Father Tommy was cured of his cancer!

Gloria

We want you to know we are thinking of you.
Hope your recovery is going smoothly, too.
Many of us are in quarantine
To avoid getting COVID-19.

Remembering your gourmet cuisine dinner,
For movie group friends, a sure winner.
Fun times sharing the latest movie on Tuesday nights,
Adventure, comedy, romance, war-time frights.

Delicious dinners at the club when golf was done.
Taking turns sharing summer plans, trips for fun.
Your calls to check up and see if we are OK
Through life's ups and downs, come what may.

Blessings, yet always more challenges we seem to face,
Adding to our retirement pace.
Miss seeing your sweet smile and gentle ways,
Listening to your stories of family days.

Praying for surgery success, comfort during healing,
Plenty of painless resting and sleeping,
And very soon you will feel brand-new,
And like the way you look, too.

My dear friend had skin cancer on her nose, several surgeries, and a
lengthy recovery. April, 2020
Her surgeries were successful and she is beautiful as always.

COVID-19

My Dearest Jeanne,
Read about you having the virus, SO SAD!
Saw you were in the hospital, SO MAD!

How does this happen? What can we do?
Wait, hope, have faith, and pray for you.
The miles have separated us two,
The Potter Clan is thinking of you.

I am sending healing thoughts your way.
Asking God for total recovery every day.
Many tears shed because of my sadness.
Stronger hope for wellness and gladness.

Every confidence in God's power as I kneel.
Every confidence in God's power to heal.
Prayers for all staff who care for you.
Strength, wellness, protection, too.

God's special protection for Nurse Renee,
And for Howard we also pray.
Prayers that you will soon see
Total recovery.

Hugs and much love from,
Ron and Linda Potter in Sarasota, FL
Jennifer, Tony, Ella, Olivia Kuper in Ankeny, IA
Jill, Jason, Shelby, Taylor, Jackson, JT Storm in Bloomington, IN

Kathy Birkett, Karyl Grecu, and family
My church prayer team, my closest neighbor friends
March 26, 2020

On Maundy Thursday, April 9, 2020, God called this very special angel home to heaven. On Easter Sunday she was wearing an Easter Bonnet, her Resurrection Crown. My tears have given way to sharing her incredible legacy. You can read about her STEP Class in Tribute Threads and her Sensational Sixty years in Birthday Threads. Jeanne was seventy-two.

Graduation Threads

Create my Tapestry

Graduation is an eventful time
For remembering and making a rhyme.
From newborn years,
Through high school cheers,
Those college ways,
Working pay days,
Memories of friends, teachers, events,
Classes, grades, sports, awards, achievements.

Notre Dame Bound

Christopher,

We watched you grow, for many years.
Shared with you our laughter and tears.

Memories of our Golden Retriever, Molly, with you.
So many times you helped with her and us, too.

Your friends playing football on backyard ground.
Running through the garden to score a touch down.

Memories of Mandy and Nora, too.
You washing your car to make it look new.

We've watched you mature into a young man.
We see how tall you proudly stand.

Successfully completing High School days.
Making right choices, that always pays.

The University of Notre Dame's acceptance of you.
Classes, sports games, exciting challenges, too.

God's blessings as you go your new way.
God's blessings each university day.

May 1996

After graduating Notre Dame University, Christopher served in the Peace Corps. He met and married Holly and they now have three children. Christopher is now a U.S. diplomat serving in Africa.

Loving Graduate,
A+ Style

October 11, 1974.
Miss Jill Marie was born, making it the Potter Four.
Jennifer would frown every time you would cry.
Dad would frown if Mom said, Check to see if she's dry,
You loved the feel of a crocheted blanket that was so funky,
And one day would become your famous Bunkie.
We patted, sang, did our best
So you would sleep and we'd get some rest.
Dad had you do pull-ups holding his finger, in bed.
Just see how strong she is and will be, he said.

The Sunday School foot and hand prints made into a turkey,
Showed how much you were growing—yes, we could see.
Those early years of Junior Olympics and gym team,
Of floor routines, vaults, and balance beams.
Of Children's Choir and special songs.
Of Bible and Sunday School programs that came along.

Piano lessons year after year.
Is that Jill playing Christmas carols we hear?
Swimming and diving, each summer's fun.
Now a life guard job, just begun.
Dancing, biking, playing outside.
Now it's, Mom, I need the car and you may ride.
Jump ropes, roller skates, a leg cast.
So much to remember from your past.

Montevideo Elementary, where your school years began.
San Ramon, California, Kindergarten teacher, a man.

Then *Central Elementary, grades one to four,*
Indianapolis, Indiana, anything but a bore.

Grades five to six, Banyon Elementary, Newbury Park, California.
Outstanding Sixth-Grade Student Award,
your name on a plaque to stay.
Remember the style show, your teacher's fancy clothes and car.
You certainly were her shining star.
Seventh and eighth were at Sequoia
Intermediate, art work honors, gee.
Your graduation photo taken with your Golden, Miss Molly.

Ninth grade, Newbury Park, cheerleading fun.
Your high school career had just begun.

But a *move to Naperville, Illinois* was really hard.
And your life seemed suddenly marred.
You were brave, strong, and bold.
Had a strong faith to which you did hold.
You conquered struggles, fought a good fight.
Your eye a new sparkle, life a new light.
Waubonsie High School track with a four
feet, ten inches in the High Jump.
A stress fracture, and in the leg, a new lump.
Third in both eight hundred relay (1:48) and medley (1:54) race.
MVP and Conference record time 4:10.6, first place.
You played volleyball for three years and club in off-season.
Lots of games and tournaments won.
Volleyball, All Conference Team and Coaches' Captain.
Trophies, medals, ribbons to gain.
As we focus on you tonight,
We see you in a different light.

To Friends, one who gives advice, sees justice done.
To Teachers, natural leader, achiever, and lots of fun.

To Dad, star athlete in any sport you think about.
To Mom, beautiful daughter both inside and out.
To Sister, best friend, wardrobe with open door.
To Grandparents, Wiggy on gym floor.

More importantly than all you've achieved,
Is the legacy and challenge you leave.
Fairness, justice, right be done.
Loyalty, faithfulness in relationships with everyone.
Your loving, caring manner, energy, smile,
Make you a *loving graduate with an A+ style.*
June 7, 1992

Jill graduated from Indiana University, married Jason, taught high school, and coached volleyball. She ran several marathons, including Chicago and Boston. Jill and Jason have raised four children. Jill is employed by Kelley School of Business, Indiana University, where two of her four children attend. She is currently enrolled in the Master's Program.

Cherished Past

October 11, 1974, it seems like only yesterday.
The birth of our second daughter, home from the hospital to stay.
Miss Jill Marie was your Baptized name.
My mind goes over what you became.
Louisville, Kentucky, your Play School Gym Bar.
Watched you flip, knew you'd go far.
Stroller ride on 4908 Ulrich Road each day.
Patted you to sleep, your special way.

Minnetonka, Minnesota, your two-wheel bike.
Feeding geese, what a cute tike.
18801 Hanus Road,
When asked where you lived, that's what people were told.
Sleeve on fire, stitches in your nose.
Broken leg, cast, knitted cover for your toes.
Circus clown pulled a quarter from your ear.
Nothing but thunder, did you fear.
Plenty of snow in which to play.
Plenty of snow from October to May.
Gymnastics at the YMCA.
Swimming at Lake Ann,
This little lady loved a tan.

San Ramon, California, roller skating in the sun.
Kindergarten and school time fun.
Pig tails or permed, your choice of hairdo.
2555 Toltec Circle you now knew.

Next Indianapolis, Indiana, and 7601 Noel Forest Lane.
So much to do, so much to gain.

Diving team at the pool.
Success in elementary school.
Sunday and Bible School, Choir at church.
You enjoyed watching birds on the feeder perch.
Ben and Elizabeth, your neighborhood friends.
Watch Jill on the gym mat bend.
Cartwheels, flips, Junior Olympic events.
Waiting for judging, were you tense?

Then *California, 923 Deer Spring Place.*
Newbury Park was a faster pace.
More gymnastics, swim team fun.
Point Mugu beach, sand, and sun.
Outstanding Six Grade Student award to you.
First Homecoming dance, fancy dress, too.
Molly came as your pet.
Cheerleading, your favorite pastime, you bet.
Teeth braces, piano practice, friends at the door.
Jill's life, never a bore.

4018 Naperville, Illinois, Broadmoor Circle, we add.
This move made Jill very sad.
Spring Break trips to Florida sun.
Waubonsie High School track meet fun.
Volleyball games filled your days.
Ace serves, winning team your ways.
High School friends, memories.
Graduation, lots of parties.

Indiana University days, IU
Special sisterhood of *Delta Delta Delta Sorority,* too.
Parent Weekends, football games.
New friends and familiar names.

Moving out and moving in.
Changing rooms in the house again.
Dad's Weekend, Mom's Weekend, too.
Time to show case what you do.
Many events happened in four, fast years.
Many smiles but some tears.

As one chapter closes, another will unfold.
Wonderful events yet untold.
Your heart will hold your cherished past.
There it will always safely last.
As we remember your life so far,
You are our bright, shining star.
May God continue to keep you in his way,
As you go forward every day.
With all our hearts, we very much love you.
And are very proud of you, too.

May you have a wonderful Senior Week!
Easter Sunday, April 7, 1996

Journal Page Discovery

Six grandchildren, Shelby was the first.
High School graduation, excitement to burst.
I found a journal page I wrote eighteen years ago.
A B C baby attributes printed here for all to know.

To Shelby   Love, Grandma Linda   December 25, 2000

Amazing Angel
Baby
Cute and content
Darling
Eyes so bright
Fascinating, focused
Girl
Healthy
Interested and inquisitive
Just perfect
Kind
Loved by all
Miracle from God

Nine pounds—almost
Our precious lady
Pumpkin
Queen Shelby
Radiant and
Soft—oh so soft
Tiny, but long fingers and toes
Unique
Very pretty
Warm and wonderful
X-tra special
Your dreams come true
Zest for life as she loves to
look around

P.S. Someday I'll update these baby attributes to a grown-up version of your A B C's.

At my daughter's home, organizing in the basement,
Discovered the journal entry, getting ready
for graduation commencement.

Inspired by my journal page attribute discovery,
Wrote an updated version as we could all see
This well-rounded graduate has many qualities.
I only had one day of time.
Unfortunately the attributes do not rhyme.

The next poem, *Graduate Shelby's A B C's*

High School Graduate Shelby's A B C's

To Shelby as she graduates
Blooming North High School

Amazing, Athlete, Adorable, Accomplished
Beautiful inside and out, loves the Beach

Caring, Competitive, Confident, Cheerleader
Darling, Daring

Eyes sparkling, Ever ready for action
Focused, Fabulous, Fashionable, Friendly, Friend

Gorgeous, Generous, Graduate, Gymnast, Granddaughter
Healthy, Hard working, Happy, Hugger

Intelligent, Interesting, IU, here I come!
Juggling a busy schedule, Job, Jeans, Joyful

Kind hearted, Keyboard, Knowledgeable
Loving, Limber, Leader, Lovely

Mature, Motherly to her cat Nala, Moral
Nice, Neat, North Graduate

Outstanding in all areas, Out going
Pretty, Pet lover, Passionate

Quick to learn, Quality, Queen
Radiant, Runner

Shelby, *Shelbers*, Spirited, Sporty, Scholar, Sweetheart
Trustworthy, Talkative, Talented

Unique, You're the only one of your kind.
Vivacious, Victorious, Vibrant

Wonderful, Warm, Water sports, Wise, Worshipful
X-tra special to all, X-citing college

Years ahead, Youthful, Yoga
Zestful, Zucchini bread lover

June 1, 2019

Success

Eighteen years of layers of life, we celebrate today,
Add up to a colorful kaleidoscope array.

Newborn feedings, toddler exploration,
School achievements and learning fun.

Sporting events, workout routines,
Your body sculptured strong and lean.

Book smarts, fabulous grades, healthy brain.
Your academic excellence was always a gain.

As you graduate, you can feel satisfied and proud.
Eighteen years to this life point, you can shout out loud.

S U C C E S S
That's the way we spell success.
But, Success is not about the car you drive.
It's about the place you're going to which you strive.
It's not about how you look in that photo on the shelf.
It's about how you see yourself.
It's not about who you know.
It's about who you are on the go!

S U C C E S S
Shelby, you are by every definition a huge success.

Loving words from Pappy and Tanny, our Shelby so dear.
From this point forward, life may not always be clear.

So stay true to your heart and let love guide your way.
Be honest and kind in all that you say.

Have faith in God's Word—just trust and obey.
And God will guide and protect you each day.

Congratulations High School Graduate June 1, 2019

Shelby was accepted to Indiana University, several
blocks from her home in Bloomington.

Bloomington High School North

Awards for Taylor Storm

Graduation, perfect time to make a rhyme.

Monroe County Sports Hall of Fame $1,000 Scholarship.
Engage, empower, educate, enrich.
One girl, one boy chosen from graduation class
Taylor chosen, no one could surpass.
In the school hall, her photo and award hung on a plaque.
Spring Sport, Girls' Field and Track

More Acclaim at *Senior Night*
Taylor once again in the *Spotlight*.
Four years, Varsity Volleyball, member of
the Student Athletic Board,
Gold Award in Volleyball, Scholar Athlete Award.
State Medalist in 4 x 400
Indoor Record holder, 4 x 200 and 4 x 400.
Outdoor Record Holder, 4 x 100 and 4 x 400.
Hoosier State Relay medalist 2018 and 2019.
This gal is focused, fast, quick, and lean.

Sophomore of the Year Award, Track and Field.
All Conference Member Volleyball, Track and Field.
Membership awarded to National Honor Society
Worked in Bloomington with Habitat for Humanity
Second Team All Area in Volleyball.
When it came to awards, Taylor took them all.
May, 2020

COVID-19 pandemic quarantine canceled prom, state track meet, and graduation commencement. Parents were determined to make something creative happen. An outdoor ceremony was planned. Pomp and Circumstance music was piped outside as students in cap and gown, paraded to folded chairs. Each of the fourteen graduates, friends since middle school, gave a speech from a podium with a microphone. Photos were taken by a flag, and all caps removed and thrown into the air to end the ceremony. Parents in attendance, video taped the ceremony to share with friends and family.

Taylor Storm, A to Z.

Many fond memories of thee.

Adorable baby, athletic lady, All-State Volleyball award.
Academic achievement for her, not hard.
Bouncing in her crib, building momentum to dive head first.
Bouncing that volleyball to serve an ace at which she is well versed.
Curly-haired little girl. Do not comb. That's the news.
Curly-haired grown-up lady, straightened in various stylish dos.
College bound, IU attire, camo pants and tennis shoes.
Christmas in Florida, then with best friend, a Caribbean Cruise.

Dimples in her darling, beautiful childhood face.
Still darling, but daring as she rounds
first base or runs her fast pace.
Daddy's girl, he helped her grow.
Where did those years rapidly go?
They drew you in, those big brown eyes.
Now *extravagant energy* instead of cries.
Fruit, all flavors, as a child she loved them best.
Now fun loving, funny, always fashionably dressed.

Granddaughter number two, born in 2002.
Now gorgeous, gluten free with great grades, too.
Healthy, happy, baby girl. Hair flowing, ponytail, braid, or swirl.
Horses and riding lessons, she gave it a twirl.
Inquisitive childhood mind amazed her kin.
Emphatic volleyball slam to secure the win.
Now *intelligent* and *interesting.*
Her internship, athletic training.

No joking, another granddaughter, another doll toy.
Jumping in volleyball for the kill, what a joy.
Taylor's two brothers, JT and Jackson,
Joined by family, love, laughter, and fun.
Kindness, a quality from heaven.
Stained glass starring Sandhill Crane baby Kevin.
Loved broccoli more than cookies baked.
Still *loving*, laughing, fun times with friends at the lake.

Mother's love and nurturing.
Baby girl matured. Go spread your wings.
Newborn, nuck, napping, cute as can be.
Nala's pantry accident, you and Tanny cleaned on hand and knee.
Notre Dame Volleyball Camp each year.
University *news*, IU bound, I did hear.
Oh how she loved to bounce on my knee
Original stained glass of Kevin designed for me.

Pudgy cheeks on that pretty face,
Called for a pinch, anytime, any place.
Stunning red prom dress her Junior year,
Purchased during Florida Spring Break while she was here.
Quiet, please. Nap time, not a peep.
Quiet water runs deep.
Relaxed, carefree.
Relay runner, fast as can be.

Swimming lessons, never to drown.
Back surgery never slowed her down.
Stable, smart, smiling, sister Shelby dear.
State Meet, sixth place, 4 x 400 relay, Junior year.

Serving spree in volleyball tied the score.
Whatever her sport, Taylor always gives more.
Teething until those first teeth beam.
Talented track star, setting school records by relay team.

Indoor State Meet times in 4 x 200, 4 x 400, never before seen.
Thinking skills and strategies, problem solving, for her a breeze.
Under the bed sheets for tents, you would hide.
Unique personality and beauty now abide.
Very difficult to rock to sleep. Versatile athlete, very vivacious.
Volleyball number six, BNHS: digs, kills, assists, aces.
Tour of the zoo on Tanny's birthdays, a fun wagon ride.
Wondering your future's wandering stride.

X-tra ordinary in her past.
X-tra special and x-tra fast.
You were always yourself, no pretense, no fear.
Coming in and being task efficient in volleyball, your Senior year.
Zip, zing, as a baby and toddler, easily fed.
Now she loves her Tanny's Zucchini Bread.

Who would have thought a Pandemic Coronavirus would end:
Senior year at school, state track meet,
prom, time spent with friends.
Then up, up, and away in a Hot Air Balloon to see more.
Just the beginning of ways, Taylor will soar!

Happy Bloomington North High School Graduation.
This time in your life, remembered as unique innovations.
If we cannot be together on Graduation Day,
We still have tons of Taylor memories, come what may.

Love, hugs, and kisses,
Prayers and best wishes!
Tanny and Pappy
May, 2020

Each letter of the alphabet, a baby or childhood
attributes first, then attributes now as a graduate.

Heritage Threads

Create my Tapestry

Looking back through the pages of time,
Help us unravel, make sense of our rhythm and rhyme.
Our parents' lives survived life's tests,
The Great Depression, a flood, World War II, giving their best.
Raising children, working long hours,
Satisfying memories and love's power.
Daily activities and family fun,
Lives lived to the fullest, vacations in the sun.
So many blessings, too many to count.
God always with us, paramount!

Linda Sue Messel Potter's parents:

Louis Irvin Messel (February 26, 1926–August 6, 2002) lived for seventy-six years.

Phyllis Mae Kanzler (October 2, 1924–December 10, 1997) lived for seventy-three years.

Irvin and Phyllis were married (August 12, 1946–December 10, 1997) for fifty-one years.

Walter Ronald Potter's parents:

Walter Potter (September 27, 1909–June 6, 1984) lived for seventy-four years.

Martha Louise Brown (December 21, 1922–February 13, 2011) was eighty-eight years.

Walter was married to Martha (August 7, 1943–June 6, 1984) for forty years.

Bernard Mills was married to Martha Potter (May 13, 1989–April 9, 2009) for nineteen years.

Forty Years of Married Life

Forty years of married life.
Forty years since Irvin took Phyllis for his wife.
Forty years since Irvin asked, Will you?
Forty years since Phyllis said, I do.
Forty years of laundry and meals.
Forty years of fixing wagon wheels.
Forty years of sewing dresses.
Forty years of cleaning up messes.
Forty years of hopes and dreams.
Forty years of plans and schemes.
Forty years of Sunday picnics in the sun.
Forty years of family vacation fun.
Forty years of games and bikes.
Forty years of church camps and hikes.
Forty years of houses and yards.
Forty years of Uno and Kanzler cards.
Forty years of dance recital review.
Forty years of dance costumes, too.
Forty years of Red Cross Swim Lesson fun.
Forty years of Hi Li Swim Club sun.
Forty years of school, homework, PTA.
Forty years of carpools, cheerleading hooray.
Forty years of practicing piano and flute.
Forty years of singing in choir to boot.
Forty years of teaching Sunday School.
Forty years of living by the Golden Rule.
Forty years of birthday breakfast in bed.
Forty years of bed time stories read.
Forty years of boyfriends and dates.

Forty years of weddings and mates.
Forty years of daughters moving.
Forty years of granddaughters grooving.
Forty years of listening to Irvin snore.
Forty years of a whole lot more.
Forty years of chocolate delight.
Forty years of Weight Watcher might.
Forty years of prayers sent.
Forty years of support lent.
Forty years of joy and love.
Forty years blessed by God above.
August, 12, 1986

Phyllis and Irvin Messel

Fortieth Wedding Anniversary

I know if your dear mother were in her right mind,
She'd want you to have a special anniversary line.

She'd want you to know, she'd want to say,
I hope you have a very special fortieth anniversary day.

All I ever wanted for you, Irvy, My Boy,
Was a life of love, happiness, and joy.

You couldn't have found anyone, who more perfectly fit the bill,
Than your beautiful, wonderful wife named Phyll.

Son, you've always made me extremely proud of you,
And of your wonderful family, too.

Phyll takes such special care of me.
She loves me like her own Mother. How can that be?

Granddaughters Connie and Linda were always such a joy.
Always good like you, Irvin, when you were a boy.

Great-granddaughters Jennifer and Jill were such darling babies.
I can't believe how quickly they've grown into such fine ladies.

And so on this your special day,
I want you to know in my own special way,

That deep down in my little heart,
You've always been a great big part.

Happy fortieth anniversary on this your special day.
May you have many wonderful years spent in your own special way!

Love Always,
Mom (Eleanor Messel Boone)

Granny and Paw Paw

Happy fortieth anniversary today,
Granny and Paw Paw, we want to say.

Wish we could be there to celebrate, too.
Know how very much we both love you.

Forty married years, we think that's great
To be married to the same mate.

We remember all the times
You gave us nickels, you gave us dimes.

You took us places where there were things to see.
Talked to us about what you hoped we'd be.

We played cards and had fun
Swimming at Hi Li Swim Club, in the sun.

Babysitting and watching us grow,
Sledding with us in the snow.

Games, stories, ice cream cones.
You wanted to put meat on our thin bones.

Coming to visit when we moved away.
Having fun and making the most of every day.

We love you. What more can we say?
We hope you have a special day.

Love, Granddaughters Jennifer and Jill
August, 12, 1986

To Irvin and Phyllis

Dad and Mom
Grandpa and Grandma
Uncle and Aunt
Husband and Wife
Friend and Lover

A faith that blesses, guides and cheers.
A wealth of memories, time endears.
A love grown richer through the years.
God be with you on your anniversary day.
And bless your life together today and always.

Happy fortieth anniversary.
Connie and Josh (Ridker)
August 12, 1986

April 2, 2020, I am home-bound due to safety requests for the coronavirus. It is the perfect time to work on my poetry. I wanted to include this poem from my sister and her husband that I was surprised to find after thirty-four years. I was typing Josh's poem into my computer, when he phoned me from Dallas, Texas. What a coincidence.

Hershey Kisses

Happy sixtieth birthday, Granny Messel.

You love us, Granny.

Oh yes, you do.

But we know you love,

Your Chocolate, too.

So we decided for your birthday wish,

To turn into a Hershey Kiss!

Much love and lots of hugs.

Granddaughters,

Jennifer and Jill
October 2, 1984

We used aluminum foil to make the Hershey Kiss costume. Toilet paper was used for the piece of paper that says, *Hershey Kiss*. The poem was actually sung as a song. We celebrated Phyllis Messel's birthday in Louisville, Kentucky, before moving from Indianapolis to California.

Big Seven Oh Birthday

Louis Irvin Messel

Irvin Messel has lived 25,500 days.
Most of them in all the right ways.
His father died when Irvin was a nine-year-old boy,
He became *the man of the house*, no time for toys.

Friends would call for him, outside to play.
He preferred reading books inside all day.
Oh what knowledge his love would acquire.
Reading every book, his only aspire.

I remember he would always say,
Get a good education, no one can take that away.
Musical talent he shared with all.
Choir singing or humming in concert hall.

Vocal range sung with power and might,
Traditionally on Christmas Eve, *Oh Holy Night.*
Directing choir on many a Wednesday,
Picking hymns that Linda could play.

Loved us daughters with fatherly pride,
By our sides would always abide.
Helped and encouraged us each step of the way.
Always wanted to know what we had to say.

Family, Sunday afternoon picnics in the park.
Sparklers on July, fourth in the night time dark.
Checked our homework every night.
Helped alleviate any fright.

Taught us the power of trusting God in our life.
Showed us how to depend on God in all strife.
With him beside us we grew strong.
His love became our confidence all along.

Watched us dance, sing, and piano play,
Swim, cheerlead, finally go our own way.
Supported us through college days,
Helping us in many ways.

Walking us down the bridal aisle,
Kissing us with a big smile.
Husbands, grandchildren, grand dogs, and grand cats.
All the fun times he grandfather sat.

Linda, Ron, Connie, Josh, Jennifer, and Jill,
The loves of his life, especially Phyll.
Forty-nine-and-a-half years Phyllis has been his wife,
Together they have lived a rewarding life.

If Granny Boone could be here today,
We know what she would say.
My boy, my only son, perfect in every way.
Have a wonderful, happy seventh birthday.

Born February 26, 1926
Celebrating his seventh, February 26, 1996

1926 Interesting Facts to Know

What can we say about Dad turning the big Seven Oh?
Here are some interesting facts to know.
Louis Irvin Messel was born on February 26,
In the year 1926.
1926 was also the year
These events occurred, you are about to hear.

Babe Ruth caught a baseball dropped from a plane.
Gertrude Ederle, first woman to swim English Channel and be sane.
Miniature Golf was invented in Tennessee.
Gene Tunney beat heavyweight boxing champ Jack Dempsey.
Byrd party made first flight over the North Pole.
Ford Motor Company started the forty-
eight-hour workweek as a goal.

First motion picture with sound was demonstrated.
Congress established the Army Air Corps it's said.
Robert Goddard fired the first liquid fuel rocket.
That was probably the beginning of the space program, I bet.
Rayon pigskin garters cost fifty cents on the store rack.
Cigarettes cost twenty cents a pack.

A half-gallon of milk cost twenty-eight cents, delivered to your door.
A Model T Ford sold for $350 at the car store.
Andy Griffith, Jerry Lewis, Bea Arthur were born in 1926.
Queen Elizabeth II, Marilyn Monroe, Joe
Garagiola, some famous picks.
First Transatlantic phone call was made.
Slide fasteners were named zippers and have stayed.

Al Capone headquarters sprayed with gunfire. No one was hurt.
New radio voices *George Burns and Gracie Allen,* what a cute flirt.
These popular books published, *The Sun*
Also Rises and *Winnie the Pooh.*
Little did you know, granddaughter Jennifer's
favorite would be Pooh, too.
These are some interesting facts to know
About the birth year of Dad who turns the *big, Seven Oh.*

Wedding Bells

She said, I've a secret
I want you to know

About a guy named Bernie
Who's become my beau.

Ruth introduced us.
That's how it began.

And now in marriage
He's asked my hand.

We have so much fun.
No matter what we do.

Life takes on a special meaning
When there are two.

May 13, 1989
Hopewell Church is the place.
2:00 p.m. is the time

And so we wish Bernie and Martha,
On this their wedding day,

Love, Joy, and Happiness,
Now and Always.

Martha's Eightieth Birthday Toast

There aren't many these days who can boast,
Reaching their eightieth birthday, so we give a toast
To Martha Louise Brown Potter Mills.
You're not allowed to add more names or pills.
We thought it might be fun to retrace,
History of this familiar face.
We look back on this incredible life,
Daughter, mother, grandmother, great-grandmother, wife.

As a little girl, one of sisters four.
Ruth, Dottie, Lillian, Martha, her parents did adore.
They would grow up to marry some day.
But none would move very far away.
Martha wed Walter in 1943
Soon they had a family of four, you see.
Three sons: Ronnie, Donnie, Dennis, too.
A girl would be nice, then Patty made that dream come true.

Because the families lived close by,
Each weekend they would always try,
To celebrate in a special way,
With aunts, uncles, cousins in the field to play.
Those growing years were busy days,
Children, farm, husband, all going different ways.
Bikes replaced diapers, ball games appeared.
PTA and school work memories to hold dear.

Flowers, gardening, canning the crops,
Filling freezer with beef, floors to mop.

Drill Team, cross-country, basketball games,
Fern Creek High School, graduation names.
Suddenly her children were all grown,
Off to make lives of their very own.
College, careers, job adventures to bring.
Wasn't long before wedding bells would ring.

Army and Navy took those husbands to different coasts.
Now there are war veterans to boast.
The Potters four each took a mate,
Soon grandchildren to celebrate.
Some moved away, some stayed in town.
More trips to visit all around.
Martha and Walter relived past days,
Joys of grandchildren in many ways.

Martha and Walter enjoyed watching the grandchildren play.
All loved the farm, having a hay day.
Then Walter died, leaving a sad void.
Forty years of marriage, they enjoyed.
Years of memories to cherish,
Life must go on, was everyone's wish.

Then along came Bernie,
He made Martha rather care free.
Bernie brought laughter, joy, and a smile,
Martha had not been happy in a while.
Martha married Bernie, hammer, saw, swing,
With wood and nails, that man can make anything.
Once again Cupid strikes with arrow and bow.
This time granddaughters' wedding bells will toll.
Tony finds Jennifer and Jason takes Jill.
Aimee and Marty's military wedding on a hill.

Soon more pitter-patter of little feet,
Great-granddaughters born, Shelby and Taylor, sweet.
Marty and Aimee with one on the way,
A great-grandson will be born, we are excited to say.

So many blessings, so many years.
Family memories, friends to hold dear.
Happy eightieth birthday Mom, Martha, Granny, too.
Thank you for helping me learn to tie my shoe.
Thank you for spouses *to have and to hold*.
Thank you for more covers when we were cold.

We give you a special eightieth birthday toast.
We're better people for knowing you, we boast.
We love you. That's all we can say.
Have a great celebration day.
December 2, 2002

Origins

Tapestry Threads, when do they begin in one's life?
As a child, as a teen, as an adult, as a wife?
When I was born, we lived with my grandparents, 678 East Lawn,
Being an island street, the house next door was on West Lawn.
Fond memories from photos taken of grandparent times.
Importance of heritage and family love that binds.

Philip and Magnolia Kanzler, when younger, played with a band.
My grandfather on the drums, granny on the piano, quick hands.
My love of music, singing round the piano, on many days
Piano, organ lessons, high school chorus, my music ways.
After Children's Choir practice at St. Mark's Church,
The organist, on her bench would perch,
She would play that organ, make it rock.
Her hands on two keyboards, her feet on the pedals, in socks.

Piano teacher, Mary Ann Lineberrie, church recitals with Miss Miller.
I was the church organist, My Dad, Irvin
Messel, was the choir director.
Retirement now gives me time for keyboard playing
Key Chorale Concerts and Church Choir anthem singing.
My husband loves to play music for us each day
And I can be heard singing along in my mighty way.
My piano given to granddaughter Olivia, who can play by ear,
In hopes that she and Ella continue the piano playing, I hold so dear.

In 1951, I was four, we moved to 1610 Sale Avenue.
We had no car, public buses or rides with friends would have to do.

Daddy rode the bus to downtown office job in the morning light.
We rode our bikes to the bus stop to meet him at night.
Even though he knew we would be there,
He always acted surprised, to beat us home on foot he would dare.

On Sundays, we would walk to the neighbor's house down the street.
Their yard filled with violets, ride to church in their car, a big treat.
For many years, riding my bike was the way I got around.
I sold my bike, needed the money, I was college bound.
I still ride my bike, great exercising, retirement fun.
I pedal to exercise and yoga classes, the swimming pool in the sun.

My Mother was never allowed to go swimming,
Because her uncle died from drowning.
Friends pushed her in the pool one day,
Thinking it a cool trick to play.
Now my Mother knew that drowning feeling,
Vowed her children would be good swimmers, her healing.
Red Cross Swim Lessons every summer
vacation, passing the tests.
Lapping, diving, life guarding, college
synchronized swimming the best.

To swim the English Channel, my high school ambition.
Three miles, the farthest distance I swam, Hi Li pool my location.
White Zinc Oxide ointment protecting my nose, in my guard chair.
My husband's first look at me, through binoculars he would stare
From across the street from the pool, before our first date.
Wet hair slicked back, was it too late, could
he guess I would be his mate?
Lapping in the swimming pool is still my therapy.
Relaxing, praying, making rhymes for my poetry.

Granny Kanzler helped me make a doll quilt one day.
She passed along her love of sewing to her daughter Phyllis Mae.
My Mother, Phyllis, was quite the seamstress, you see.
Polka-dot material purchased, became Easter dresses for three,
Friends at church saw us coming, I think we are seeing spots.
Is it our eyesight, or are there lots of colorful dots?
That polka-dot material just did not look
right for a dust ruffle for the bed,
Being very frugal, my Mother made dresses instead.

I sewed a gathered skirt, in high school Home Economics class,
Mother helped me make a matching top,
the outfit looked like a dress.
She made all the bridesmaids dresses for my wedding day.
I have followed in the footsteps, thread,
needles, patterns along the way.
I stitched coats, hats, swim suits, dresses, outfits for my ladies,
Chair cushion and toy box covers, shower curtains, draperies.
Sewed many a garment over the years.
To my mother and grandmother I give the cheers.

I was born a teacher at heart.
As a young girl, playing school in the garage, I got my start.
Charles D. Jacob, Okolona Elementary,
Southern High, Murray University.
Studied hard, scholarships awarded,
achieved that teaching degree.
I remember walking to school, getting bit
by a dog, friends I would see.
Getting hot water for my teacher for
soaking her nails or making tea.
U.S. Savings Stamps purchased at school, left behind.
My teacher brought them to our home as we sat to dine.

Mother was president of the PTA. Raised
money for our school, in her day.
Mr. Reid, my first male teacher in sixth grade,
His high school son, in the marching band, the tuba he played.
During school recess we liked to Hula-
Hoop, on the swing set, swing high.
A boy burned a hole through his jeans with
a mirror and sunlight from the sky.
My parents built a new house, to the new
school my Mom would drive.
We would eat and change clothes in the closet, then dance lessons
to jive. 8012 White Cedar Drive, in 1959, our new address would be
My sister, Connie, and I had our own rooms, happy finally.

I loved playing school, teaching my friends, getting facts fixed.
I taught Sunday School, swimming lessons,
grades preschool through sixth.
My own tutoring business, the *Learning*
Academy, where learning is fun.
Assisting grandchildren with sports skills in the Florida sun.
Indiana, California, Illinois for many years in Bible Study Fellowship.
Graduate Workshops, studying, learning,
teaching, lecturing, leadership.
Retirement now, but learning is never done.
I enjoy learning and helping friends play Mah-Jongg.

My family was the first on our street to own
a black-and-white television, TV.
Mom opened a window, Dad turned the TV,
so all the neighbors could see.
Each year we took a vacation, made a
scrapbook from our travel log.
My sister and I took turns copiloting,
figuring gas mileage, singing songs.

We learned about our parents' lives as, *Mares Eat Oats*, they sang.
Down by the Ole Mill Stream and states songs rang.
Where has Or-e-gon? She's gone to pay her Tex-as.
What did Dela-ware? She wore her New Jersey.
We played memory games, rhyming games that made travel fun.
All our vacations were by automobile,
educational, not just in the sun.
Lived in six different states, spectacular sections of our country.
Traveled the world, amazed by the sights of land and sea.
Retirement has brought cruises and trips to be with family.

I began dance lessons when I was eight,
taking a tap and ballet combo,
JoAnn Doll and her Dancing Dolls, lessons in her basement studio.
Recitals with fancy costumes at Memorial Auditorium in Louisville.
Grandparents would come, pictures taken, such a girl thrill.
One year, costumes fell out of the seamstress's open car trunk.
My dad went looking and retrieving to save the day with luck.
When we moved, I changed studios.
I was hired to help teach, studied tap,
ballet, jazz, ballroom, and toe.
We Hula-Hooped, jitter bugged in a downtown
store window on Fourth Street,
My dancing pictures were in the newspaper several times, so sweet.
Retirement, still a dancing queen,
Enjoy the grandkids' videos of their modern dancing scenes.

Church and prayer were always a big part of my life.
As a child, I prayed for Christmas, my friend would get a bike.
Mom said, *God hears, answers prayers of a believing heart.*
The friend's father had no job, Mom feared as my prayers did start.
Christmas morning on the front porch, a bike did appear.
I have prayed diligently every day since, every day of every year.

I later learned, a bike shop owner, lived nearby,
Generously gave so a young boy wouldn't cry.

On Good Friday, my mother always hoped for weather dreary
To remind us of the sadness felt by disciples and Mary.
Our family enjoyed the fellowship of regular church dinners.
My Mom's congealed salads were always a winner.
A Jell-O salad made on the same day a jelly jar lid went missing,
The jar lid was in the middle of the Jell-O
mold salad, embarrassing finding.
Sunday School pins awarded for perfect attendance each year,
In hopes of encouraging all to attend and learn with no fear.
A gentleman with pins linked together
all the way down his suit lapel
Slept in the back pew during church every week, pray tell.

My Mother not only believed in regularly going,
She believed in staying involved, worshipping, teaching, and serving.
A pastor once said, *Pray not just for small
things, but big things as well.*
I began praying for a husband, soon after met Ron, who was swell.
*My parents set the example, helped mold me.
Retirement, but still feel the need, in service through church, to be.*

Remember When

Fun times with Linda's grandparents
My grandfather, Phillip Kanzler, did the grocery shopping
When I would go along, we would end up being
On the candy aisle, where he would look so surprised, and say,
Guess you are just going to have to pick your favorites for today.
My Mother seldom bought extras so that was always a treat.
We would buy Chocolate Stars for Granny, she loved sweets.

Granny (Magnolia) Kanzler would make biscuits for breakfast.
What makes the butterfly? She would ask.
Hot biscuits, of course the answer.
Loved those biscuits with strawberry jelly and melted butter.
At home we only had grape jelly
So strawberry was quite a treat, you see.

Grandfather (Louis) Messel, drove a family business laundry truck.
Getting out of his truck on a Friday, by a car he was struck.
In the hospital Saturday, died on Sunday.
That year, Sunday, May 12, 1935 was Mother's Day
And my Grandmother's birthday.
My Father was only nine years old when he
dealt with the death of his dad.
His Grandmother Flamm moved in to help, how sad.
Mother Eleanor had to get a job. My dad
liked to read and stay inside.
No one could convince him to play outside.
My grandmother, Eleanor Messel, would remarry one day.
Charles Boone, her friend across the street, they say.

Granny Boone had a kitchen walk-in pantry.
She would let us play with the dried beans, you see.
We would be happy for hours measuring,
Using cups and carefully spooning.
Those different colored beans mixing,
And pretending to be cooking.
Fond memories in my mind to stay
To warm my heart most any day.

Remembering Stories

As a little girl, I loved time spent at my Grandmother's house.
In the big swing, on her front porch, I would sit quiet as a mouse.
Tell me times my mom got in trouble when she was my age.
My grandmother loved telling stories, as she set the stage.
Seems a fight started between my mom and her sister.
Their bedrooms were upstairs across the hall from each other.
So their Dad (my grandfather) decided to see
The reason for the yelling, what could it be?
The sisters had begun throwing shoes at each other's room
As their Dad (my grandfather) crept upstairs to zoom
In on the ensuing quarrel and what was being said,
When a flying shoe hit him in the head.
Needless to say,
For the sisters, not a good day!

My grandparents Magnolia and Phillip Kanzler
My mother, Phyllis, her sister, Joyce, my aunt

During The Great Flood of 1937, in Louisville, Kentucky
Rained twenty inches in January, underwater,
70 percent of the city.
When the house flooded, my mother was twelve years of age.
The family moved to a near by church to be dry and safe.
Rescuing their dog, Cinders, she moved to the church, too.
My mother's job was to potty Cinders each day,
So to the church steps she would make her way.
The church had a basement above ground,
So many steps to the church sanctuary level did abound.
Mother would walk down to water's edge, at lowest step,
Holding Cinders over the water, hoping for success.

As the flood waters rose, the steps became covered.
Each day, fewer steps, as over the water Cinders hovered.
Flood waters stopped rising with only one step left.
As prayers were answered, everyone in that church with joy leapt.

Before the flood, church youth group not allowed to play
Favorite dice game, Bunco, on leader's prize
dining room table, for display.
Ruined during the flood, lesson to learn, priorities to face.
Guess what youth group did once new table was replaced?
Played Bunco all night!
Fellowship with youth, all was right.

Daddy Tell Us

Daddy, tell us about when you were a little boy.
Did you ride your bike, have a special toy?

My Daddy, Louis Irvin Messel, was named after
His Uncle Irvin and Louis, his father.

Irvin Messel was born February 26, 1926,
Loved to stay indoors, read books for his fix.
Because his father was killed when Irvin was nine,
His mother had to work full time.
As long as Irvin was reading inside, staying out of trouble,
His mother was happy to have him in a safe bubble.

He attended a private Lutheran School.
One room, all grades, twelve students, how cool.
Dad was a smart, quiet student, a teacher's perk.
The teacher allowed him to help other students with class work.

Daddy, tell us about when you did something bad.
Did your Mother get really mad?

One time when helping get ready for dinner,
Irvin was going to fill the drink glasses, be a winner.
Instead he dropped the entire gallon of milk on the floor.
Clean up was an enormous chore.
His Mother never said a word of guff.
Cleaning up spilled milk was punishment enough.

Dad, tell us about how you met Mother.
Were you ever in love with another?

During years before Dad could drive, other guys would date Phyllis.
They would drive her by Dad's house, just to make him jealous.
Irvin took Phyllis on a date, stopped for Hot Fudge Sundaes, yes!
He tripped, spilling the Sundaes on Mom's white dress.
Phyllis was the love of Irvin's life.
WW II couldn't end soon enough so he could make her his wife.
Married on August 12, 1946

Messel Sayings

A stitch in time saves nine.
Waste not, want not, not even a dime.

A penny saved is a penny earned.
Apply zinc oxide on your nose to avoid a sun burn.

We know not what the future holds,
But we do know who holds our future.

Don't ask of others unless you
Are willing to do it yourself, too.

Drink your milk for healthy bones and teeth.
Eat Salmon and oatmeal at least once a week.

Be known for who you are, not for what you do.
Don't lower yourself to others' standards, too.

What made you popular in high school
Might not make you popular in college, as a rule.
Always stay your sweet self, rather than be cool.

When all else fails, try chocolate!

My parents, Phyllis and Irvin Messel

Messel Vacations

Guess the State Name

What did I O WEIGH (Iowa)?
She weighed a Washing-ton.
Where has O Re Gone (Oregon)?
He's gone to pay his Taxes (Texas).

Why did Cali-phone-you? (California)?
She phoned to say Ha-wai-i (Hawaii).
What did Tenne-see? (Tennessee)
She saw what Arkan-saw. (Arkansas)

How did Flori die (Florida)?
She died of Misery (Missouri).
What did Dela-wear (Delaware)?
She wore her New Jersey.

How is Louis Anna (Louisiana)?
I'll ask her (Alaska).
Who can Color ado (Colorado)?
I think Michi can (Michigan).

What did Ida ho?
She hoed her Mary land.
How did Wiscon sin?
He drank a Minne sota.

What did Connecti cut?
He cut his New Ham shire.
Why was Ill annoyed (Illinois)?
He was annoyed because of Kans sass.

We would play this game in the car while driving on vacations,
along with a math game called Buzz, and other rhyming games.

When Did the Rhyming Begin?

and keep on going. . .

My daughter asked, *When did you write your first rhyme?*
Do you remember the reason, recall the time?

Childhood and Teen Years:
Was it playing Telegram, the parlor writing game,
Extended family gathered for celebration, fun to acclaim?
Write a sentence at top of paper. Fold
paper to cover what you wrote.
At the end of that fold, write the last
word of the sentence you wrote.
To your right, pass the folded paper undisturbed.
That person writes a sentence rhyming with your last word.
That sentence ends the rhyme. Fold paper to cover your rhyme.
Do not write the last word of your sentence this time.
Game continues, then what fun, you see.
To read the silly rhymes written by family.

Was it rhyming games played, traveling in the car?
Did I make rhyming entries in our travel log on trips near or far?

Adult Life:
Was it the teacher in me, early on playing
school in a garage, realizing
For students, more fun and easier to learn if it is rhyming?

Was it that first time I did not have a card
Wrote a rhyming message. Was I a bard?

Sometimes I did have a card to send
Usually included rhyming lines I penned.
Friends and family liked the fun in the rhyme.
And wanted more over time.

Was it because I kept moving away?
For important occasions wanted to say,
Family and friends, I took the extra time,
To make a special rhyme,
In my thoughts, you always stay,
Even though I cannot be with you today.

Tanny's Thirteen

Always eat breakfast at morning light.
Say your prayers at bedtime every night.

Give Someone a sunny day.
Do something to make God smile on your way.

Take your vitamins. Be your best.
Go to bed early. Get a good night's rest.

Do something fun and enjoyable each day.
Feed your passion in that way.

You are what you eat, from your head to your feet.
You are what you read, so be careful, take heed.

You are what you see, so look carefully.
You are what you hear, clean out your ear.

You do not know what the future holds,
But you do know who holds your future.

My favorite Shakespearean quote is from *Hamlet*.
Polonius in *Hamlet* says,
To thine own self be true
And it shall follow as day follows night,
Thou canst not to anyone be false.
That we know is right.

When asked what I wanted to be called by my first grandchild, I chose *Granny*. However, Shelby, could not make the *gr* sound. My name came out as *Tanny*. All six grandchildren, many of their friends, and their parents call me *Tanny*.

Angels Watch

Jennifer, go to sleep.
Angels watch and angels keep
Over you until the sun shines through.
Mom and Daddy love you, too.

Hug your Pooh, Oh hug your Pooh.
Hug your Pooh the whole night through
Until morning sun shine wakes you two.
Now go to sleep, my Love.

I sang this poem prayer to a made-up tune, over my first born daughter, Jennifer, every night at bedtime. A Winnie the Pooh Bear was the first stuffed toy in her crib, and she became very attached to it. Over the years, as one bear wore out, we replaced Pooh with newer models. Written in 1972, this is the oldest poem in *My Tapestry of Life* book. Two years later, Jill Marie was born, and so the second verse of my lullaby changed.

Jill Marie, go to sleep.
Angels watch and angels keep
Over you until the sun shines through.
Mom and Daddy love you, too.

Hug your Bunkie, Oh hug your Bunkie.
Hug your Bunkie the whole night through
Until morning sun shine wakes you two.
Now go to sleep, my Love.

Jill became attached to a blanket called Bunkie. She carried it around for years. I attached a small piece to her wedding garter as the something old.

At Jennifer and Tony's Wedding Rehearsal dinner, I sang the lullaby one last time with the second verse changed once again. October 22, 1999

Jennifer, go to sleep.
Angels watch and angels keep
Over you until the sun shines through.
Mom and Daddy love you, too.

In the morning when you wake,
Wedding vows you now will take.
And the love that you've had for your Pooh,
Now will go for Tony, too.

Hug your Tony, Oh hug your Tony,
Hug your Tony your whole life through.
May morning sunshine always wake you two.
Blessings to you both, my Loves.

Holiday Threads

Create my Tapestry

What fun to have a holiday.
Time for sport, time for play.
Time off work, time to stay.
Time to travel, time to say,
Let's be happy, come what may.
Gather, celebrate, remember the reason,
Special friends, family, for the season.

Holidays, our Heritage

New Year, new goals, new dreams,
New hopes, new changes, new schemes.

We commemorate a day to honor *Martin Luther King*.
How valiantly he fought for equality to bring.

Groundhog Day, Punxsutawney Phil his shadow to see?
If no shadow, an early spring there will be.

Valentine love expressed in creative ways.
Valentine love rekindles sparks, they say.

Presidents' Day, how many can you name?
A country to serve and preserve and bring fame.

Easter Sunday, the stone was rolled away.
Hallelujah! He is risen today!

Mother's Day, Appreciation shown to Mothers of all ages.
Loving and guiding children through different life stages.

Memorial Day, remembering those saved, those lost.
Fourth of July, remembering freedom's blessings, freedom's cost.

Father's Day, appreciation shown to Fathers far and near.
Who worked hard to support and lead their families dear.

Labor Day, honoring all who work to make our nation great.
Thank you to those who sacrifice, spouses and mates.

Columbus Day, Columbus, in the Americas, arrived October 12, 1492.
Other explorers and settlers to follow soon.

Halloween, costumes, trick-or-treat candy, children believe.
Religious celebration for All Saints' Eve.

Veterans Day, for those who fought so I could be free.
Recount their bravery and courage for all to see.

Thanksgiving, harvest crops, gather grain for bread.
Gratitude for variety and abundance of foods we're fed.

Christmas, carols sung, cards sent, Holy Night Nativity.
Time to gather close together with friends and family.

New Year's Day

New Year's Day, a brand new year.
What passions do I hold dear?
Blank calendar pages,
Different life stages.
How will I fill the hours and minutes?
Important issues or tiny tidbits.
How will I choose to spend my days?
So many choices, too many ways.
There are twenty-four hours in each day,
There are thirty-six hours of choices in my way.
More reflection time to recall,
Past year victories or downfalls.
How many blessings can I count?
Which projects are most paramount?
Schedule time for your passions,
Time for more, time to ration.
Balance time for work and play.
Meditate, relax each day.
Give priorities the first choice.
Before minor options take voice.
Calendar pages tell your story.
So fill your days for more glory.

June, 2020

Happy Valentine's Day

✑

Happy Valentine's Day, to Alan and Cindy.

This poem is short and sweet, not long and windy.

You both give a deeper meaning to the word LOVE,

Guided by your heart, sacrifice, and God above

Always reaching out to those around you.

Visiting, helping, encouraging, too.

When there are times you don't know what to say,

Remember, Love will always find a way.

You have become very close, special friends.

The four of us together, make a great blend.

We are grateful for the friendship we share.

It makes the good days better, the bad days easier to bear.

As we celebrate Valentine's Day with husband and wife

Together we've loved our spouses 36,865 plus days of our life.

Happy Valentine's Day
February 14, 2020

ℛ

Acrostic Valentine Poem, Honey

Valentine, Be Mine, yesterday, today, tomorrow, always.

Admired, Affectionate, Athletic, Attentive, Awesome in many ways.

Love, All mine, for you, forever and two days.

Exercised your muscles to rehab and enhance your body for life.

New car electronics to program, learn and explain to your wife.

Tall, truthful, trustworthy, tasteful, tenacious, terrific, tan as can be.

Interested in orchids, cacti, pineapple plants, a wide variety.

New information from iPad, articles, and books, always learning.

Energetic, Enticing, Earnest, Ever ready a friend to be helping.

Always fun on Valentine's Day,
To stop and remember our special way,
We've loved each other throughout the years.
Happy Valentine Cheers.
February, 14, 2020

Valentine Wishes

Love of my life
Husband and Wife

Hugs and kisses
Mr. and Mrs.

Memories of fun
Laughter and sun

Ups and downs
Smiles and frowns

But always
Love abounds.

Valentine's Day
Time to say

Once each year
To us a cheer

Love of my life
Your adoring wife.

You're my Valentine each day.
You're my Valentine always.

Easter

From Bethlehem's manger to Calvary's cross.
From straw-strewn cradle to crucifixion loss?
From starlight of birth to death's darkest night.
From stone-cold tomb to resurrection light.

Early morning, the women went alone.
Surprised to discovered the rolled-away stone.
Comforted by an Angel who appears.
I know you seek Jesus, but have no fears.

When they first see Jesus, they worship Him,
On their knees, at His feet, no longer grim.
To the disciples they went, as were told,
Sharing their joyful news, afraid, yet bold.

Butterfly struggles, strengthen by strife.
Jesus is still the Resurrection Life!
Jesus is alive. He's risen today.
The stone is forever rolled away.

I died with Jesus, on Calvary's cross.
But rose from the grave, my life is no loss.
By His blood, my sins are washed white as snow.
Forgiven, redeemed, to new life I go.
No matter what challenges come what may
Belief in Jesus always wins the day.
Believe in Jesus, live eternally.
The Easter message, is truly for me.
April 12, 2020

Memorial Day

Remember lost life
        lost loved ones
        liberty
        new life

Reflect on fighting
        freedom
        flag

Remind yourself of soldiers
        surrender
        sacrifice
        service
        survival

Revisit battles
        brotherhood
        bravery

Recall price
        pain
        purpose
        promise

Mommy, Mom, Mother, Tanny

June 23,1972, the birth of Miss Jennifer Renee Potter,
Made me an official, genuine, first-time *Mother*.
October 11, 1974, Miss Jill Marie made it a family of four.
My two precious daughters, I did adore.
To them I was *Mommy*, those busy little girls,
Sesame Street, Mr. Rogers, a perm for curls.

Then I became *Mom*, I need dinner for two,
Sports activities, practices, I need new shoes.
Science projects, math facts, state capitals, teeth braces,
Outfits for spring break and new prom dresses.

Moving with Father's career presented new challenges.
New friends, good neighbors helped with our passages.
Graduation wishes, college choices,
Roommate friendships, sorority voices.
And then one day the date that came through our door
I just knew would be something much more.
Mother, I need a veil and wedding dress,
Invitations, music, venue, flowers, please no stress.
Jill's engagement event atop the Sears Tower that night
Two people in love with smiles so bright.
Jen's wedding, her first-grade class, at the alter, singing.
Bubbles, trolley ride, such fun bringing.

Then when I thought life couldn't get any better,
Membership in the Grandmothers Club forever.
Shelby had trouble saying the *GR* sound.
Granny became *Tanny*, to this day abounds.

Taylor, Jackson, Ella, Olivia, JT
Each grandchild unique as can be.
Happy Mother's Day.
Let's celebrate forty-eight years as Mommy,
Twenty years as Tanny, today.

May 10, 2020

Daddy, Dad, Father, Pappy

❦

June 23, 1972, the birth of Miss Jennifer Renee Potter,
Made you an official, genuine, first-time *Father.*
October 11, 1974, Miss Jill Marie made it a family of four.
Your two precious daughters, you did adore.
To them you were *Daddy,* those busy little girls,
Playing outdoors, swinging, leaves in their curls.

Then you became *Dad,* I need the car keys.
Dates, dances, friends, activities, the keys please.
Home work projects, sporting events, graduations.
Family fun, spring break, and summer vacations.

You were the family rock, supporting us well.
Working, traveling with your job, you were swell.
Somewhere along the way you became *Father.*
Into your daughter's life, was there another?
Please, will you walk me down the aisle?
Please no tears, only your best smile.
Two beautiful brides, perfect wedding days.
Two endearing sons by marriage, new life ways.

Everyone relied on *Father* for all kinds of advice.
You were always there with an answer to suffice.
Then in early morning hours, Shelby's birth made us happy.
Grandparents Club, your new name became *Pappy.*
Suddenly life took on new rhythm and rhyme
New adventures, exciting times.

Taylor, Jackson, Ella, Olivia, JT made six.
Each grandchild unique, added to the mix.
Today we celebrate the forty-eight years you have been a *Daddy*.
We celebrate the twenty years you have been a *Pappy*.
Happy Father's Day
May you celebrate in a special way.
June 21, 2020

Fourth of July

On this fourth of July,
Let us think about our very core.
Are we grateful for:

Freedoms we share,
The military and burdens they bear?
The right to bear arms,
To protect our families from harm?

Battles and Wars fought,
Compromises and Peace Treaties sought?
Presidents, elected officials, and laws,
Courts, government buildings, and historic halls?

Independence fought for and won,
A country where we can live, work, travel, and have fun?
Religious freedoms to read, study and pray,
Any where, any time, any day?

Educational opportunities that learning can bring,
The sports, the arts, and music to sing?
Our flag of red, white, and blue,
Our National Anthem sung often too?

On this fourth of July 2019,
We pause to remember what all of this means.
May the God in whom we trust,
Receive our thankfulness, a must.

July 4, 2019

Fourth of July

Once again we ask why?
A little history
For you and me.

Revolutionary War, April, 1775
Radical colonists pushing for the dive.
Their strong desire for independence.
By next year, Thomas Paine had written Common Sense.
A five-man committee formed to attain.
A statement justifying a break with Great Britain.

Written largely by Thomas Jefferson, their pick.
Our Declaration of Independence was adopted in 1776,
On July 4, by the Continental Congress.

John Adams (MA) and Thomas Jefferson (VA)
Were on that Committee
Both died on July 4, 1826, fifty years later.
The Declaration of Independence's, fiftieth anniversary.

Fourth of July. Today we ask why?
COVID-19 quarantine
Do you know someone whose life was:
Changed, rearranged,
Decreased, deceased,
Fearful, dreadful.
Country in disarray.
Many lives in dismay.
Lack of respect.
Total disconnect.

Healing, blessings,
Friends support,
Fears abort.
Prayers for peace.
Hope our release.
Stronger will.
Freedom still.
July 2020

Christmas Time

A little poem, a little rhyme,
Because it's Christmas time.

What kind of gift should we take?
Something to eat like a Christmas cake?
Christmas sweaters to match or new boots?
Games, books, electronics, or bathing suits?

Of maybe they would love a vacation trip,
So in the ocean they could jump and dip.
Here's a Christmas check for you to take
To pay for a trip over your summer break.

Or whenever you decide to come for fun
To relax with Tan and Pap in the Florida sun.
Our goal is always for you to know
Just how much we love you so.

In our hearts we hold you dear
And look forward to having you near.
Decide on a date when you can come stay
We will have fun every day.

Merry Christmas and Happy New Year.
We are so blessed to be with you here.
Kupers, December 25, 2017

Galena Hills

Get ready for a Spa Day.
Yea. Yea. Yea.
Jennifer, Mom, and Jill
Are off to the Galena Hills.
Our stay will begin
At the Stoney Creek Inn.
There's a fire in the fire place.
Stuffed black bear to greet you face to face.
The Irish Pub for dinner
With music, always a winner.
While food the waitress is bringing,
We are entertained with singing.
Next day we'll shop and dine,
Relax with chocolate and wine.
At the Clover Spa we'll be
Enjoying each other's company.
Toes and nails will get a manicure.
We'll be pampered, that's for sure.
Maybe dinner at Fried Green Tomatoes
And that's the way our day goes.
We relax, then head for home on Sunday.
To spend a weekend, what a fun way.
So hope your *Get-A-Way* will be great
As you redeem your certificate.
Merry Christmas.
2013 and 2014

Gift Riddle From Santa

To Olivia and JT

This gift is for you, but should be,

Shared with all in the room who want to see

Just how creative they can still be.

There is one more present you *detectives* must find.

It is not in the room in which you dine.

Nor is it in the room with a piano.

Or in the room where there could be a fire aglow.

It is in a room in the back of the house,

Where students study quiet as a mouse.

Go to that room, search, and do not stop.

The surprise is in something with a lid on top.

Both grandchildren are the same age, love puzzle solving and Mind Craft designing. They had fun searching for the gift, Legos, found in a bedroom converted into my tutoring business, The Learning Academy, where I met with students to study. JT and Olivia enjoyed the negative attributes in the poem. They spent several days creating New Year's Day floats, army vehicles, and other lego creations. Other family members had fun as well, getting down on the carpet to design. December 25, 2013

Merry Christmas

Now that we live far away,
And it's not easy to come visit just any day,

We still want you to see Tanny and Pappy.
That would make us so very, very happy.

So your Christmas gift is $$$$ for
Plane tickets as driving is a chore.

Or, if there is some other need,
Use it as you wish indeed.

Our goal is always for each of you to know
Just how very much we *love* you so.

Merry Christmas and Happy New Year.
In our hearts we hold each of you dear.

When grandparents live in Sarasota, Florida, a money gift seems to be the best way to entice family to come visit Spring Break. One daughter and her family of four, reside in Iowa. Our other daughter and her family of six, live in Indiana. Flying is a time saving, fun option for travel.

A Rhyming Christmas Letter

Make new friends, but keep the old. The one is silver, the other gold.
We are counting our blessings this time of year,
Our family and friends both far and near.
Hoping to hearing from each of you,
As we share this year's memories too.
Linda sang, *God Bless America*, at the Wounded Warrior event,
Remembering all veterans and how much our freedom meant.

Storm family arrived for Spring Break fun.
Pool, hot tub, golf cart, beach tanning in the sun.
Taylor was in Costa Rica on a mission trip.
Counselor for poor students and waterfall dip.

Linda broke her ankle with a kitchen fall.
Crutches, walking cast, lots of help from all.
Ron's eye had a retinal tear.
Laser surgery, weeks of rest, a successful repair.

A Cape Cod trip to celebrate Linda's seventieth birthday.
Surprise! Jen, Jill, Dianne, and sister Linda arrived that same day.
Thank you Karen for hosting.
Fabulous time had by ladies who are still boasting.

Every Tuesday is movie night,
With friends we see a movie and have a dinner bite.
Friends helped us celebrate Ron's seventy-second birthday.
Delicious dinner with dessert goodies, a fun way.

Watched Taylor's volleyball tournament
at the ESPN center in Orlando.
Storms returned to Sarasota for summer
fun and to the beach did go.
JT completed all five courses at Tree-Umph Park.
Extreme obstacle challenges, no lark.
Shelby did yoga with Tanny one day,
Jackson and JT on the basketball court would play.

In Des Moines, Olivia was celebrating her absolute love for art.
She received an award, for her drawing on display,
at the downtown Festival by the mart.

Our Heritage Oaks golf course was closed
for seven months renovation.
Chairman Ron in charge, from architect
planning stage to final completion.
Weekly meetings, revision of plans,
Checking on work progress, Ron was always on hand.
Ribbon-cutting speeches on opening day.
Fabulous golf course, compliments would say.

August we took a trip to get away from the heat.
See the grandkids and enjoy their beat.
Ankeny, Iowa, first stop to enjoy the Kuper crew.
Botanical gardens, butterfly house, too.
Fun sculptures made from ocean trash.
Toured a twelve-story tree house that was a smash.

Water park tubing fun in the sun.
Farmer's market shopping untill day was done.
Auto and Aircraft show with Vietnam jeep.
Grilling dinner outside, memories to keep.
Pontoon boat on the lake.

Pappy fishing, Tanny paddle boarding, a great day it did make.
Visited cabin and farm where Ella shot her first deer and turkey.
Had a snack of beef jerky.

Ella plays volleyball on her school team,
With Tony's coaching, she's a soccer queen.
Olivia enjoys piano practicing.
Outstanding soloist medal for her percussion playing.
Award for an essay she wrote in literature,
How a book she read helped her mature.
Jen and Tony are the wind beneath the family's wings.
They handle everything life brings.

Next stop Bloomington, Indiana, to see the Storm crew.
And Roscoe, their new dog, too.
Swimming with Shelby at IU's natatorium pool.
She's driving now and that is cool.
Cheerleading, child care job, Junior year studies,
Off-campus business internship, Shelby says, *more time please.*
Sophomore Taylor plays on the Varsity Volleyball team.
Her spikes and serves are mean.
The Storm sisters took North H.S. *by Storm,*
Winning track meets with perfect form.
Eighth-grade Jackson loves football and basketball plays.
Jackson can be seen scoring points for his team on game days.
The team dresses in nice pants, shirt, and tie on game day,
Building team spirit that way.
Sixth-grade JT plays football and is the place kicker.
He is a right-handed halfback but left-foot field goal kicker.
His youth football team had an undefeated season,
JT scoring seventy-five percent of the points, being the reason.
JT awarded the MVP after the championship game,
Which took place at Indiana University football stadium.
Jill and Jason work full-time jobs all the while.
Their City Church is inspiration for their style.

Friends helped secure our home,
While on vacation we continued to roam,
As Hurricane Irma was ready to hit.
Thankfully no damage, not one bit.
Louisville visit with Ron's sister Pat and Steve.
They helped us weather the storm, long
distance. It was hard to leave.
Back to Bloomington we were sent,
To enjoy more Storm crew sporting events.

Ron faced medical challenges that began on vacation.
He is still waiting for some solutions.
Sudden Hearing Loss meant deafness in his left ear.
High-tech hearing aids now help Ron hear.
Pneumonia and lung fluid, more medications to take.
Ron's vacation was no *piece of cake.*

He returned home for left leg groin angioplasty,
So he could walk without pain, you see.
Blockage in his left leg vein improved somewhat.
A stent placed in another vein in his gut.
Blood work showed low iron count which meant,
Many hours with the hematologist spent.
Blood samples and bone marrow test,
Iron Vitamins and plenty of rest.
A pulmonology appointment is pending,
To get a remedy for his problem breathing.

Linda sings in the church choir, with
practices every Wednesday night.
She sang with the Key Chorale, one hundred voices
plus symphony, in their open concert invite.
Swimming, water aerobics, and yoga keep her fit.
Her zucchini bread is still a hit.

357

To satisfy her love of teaching,
She volunteers at a local school as a tutor for reading.

Ron's sister Pat and husband Steve,
Visited Sarasota and didn't want to leave.
Botanical Garden orchids a delight.
Seafood most every night.
Bird-watching discovered forty names for our list,
Celery fields and ponds with new twists.
Beach days relaxing in the sun.
Big Cat Habitat rescue sanctuary fun.

Happy forty-ninth anniversary.
Linda made a calendar so each month to see
A photo from their wedding day,
As they celebrate the sixteenth of each monthly, in a special way.

May 2018 hold Hope, Health, Love, Joy, and Peace.

Potpourri Threads

Textures Added to my Tapestry

Assortment, collection, interesting medley.
Mixture of poems, don't fit anywhere easily.
When mixed together, they will bring
Unexpected sweet fragrances, a song to sing,
A smile to last during your day,
Or memory stirred along your way.

Because Every One Helped Out

From Crown Point to Bloomington
The Storm Crew Six moved, every one.

Friends and neighbors were sorry to see them go,
God had a different plan, the next act of their show.

Four trucks filled with the Storm stuff,
Would soon put all in quite a huff.

Boxes stacked everywhere.
Could anyone meet the dare?

Karen Keane came all the way from Boston
To help with the unpacking in Bloomington.

Karen had fond memories of her four sons in Jill's sitter care,
She offered to come and in the unpacking, share.

Tanny, (the grandmother) also arrived upon the scene.
She and Karen worked magic to unpack, organize, clean.

Jill gave the orders and boxes flew.
By day three we had paired up every shoe.

The house was livable by day five.
And everyone was still alive.

There were photos taken for album pages
To show the unpacking saga of the ages.

And how this unpacking came about,
Because every one helped out.

Delta Delta Delta Sorority

D ear and
E nduring
L ove
T hat spans
A ny situation.

D eveloping qualities,
E ver-present and
L ingering memories,
T hat
A dd joy to life.

D eep and
E ever
L asting
T rust.
A lways sisters in a special

S isterhood. A
O neness
R esulting
O nly in unity. A
R ichness added
I n
T hese university
Y ears.

Jill 1996

362

Alpha Chi Omega

Alpha Chi. My oh my.
Chosen sorority. For Miss Shelby.
Fun day. Great college way.

Junior Betsy, her Big Sister.
In high school, they cheered together.
Crown Point friends will also be
In the same sorority.
Emma, a Freshman, her sister a Junior,
Now best friends are sisters forever.

Grandmother Shannon and Aunt Jane,
Part of the celebration, a sisterhood to gain.

Special activities for Mom's Weekend.
Mothers and Daughters, time together to spend.

World's Greatest College Weekend, Little 500,
The largest collegiate bike race in the U.S., it's said.
Modeled after the Indianapolis 500, bikers compete.
Men, bike fifty miles, women, twenty-five, last year's time to beat.
Shelby is prepping for this year's race,
Sponsored by her sorority, and other bikers helping her pace.

Shelby's happiness warms our heart
With Greek choices that are smart.

January 22, 2020

COVID-19 cancelled the Little 500.
Shelby is biking and training for May, 2021.

Parkinson's Disease

Has robbed my sister of all pleasure.
Brings torture beyond all measure.
Caused mental anguish, delusions,
Frozen feet, hallucinations.

Resulted in accusations against her spouse,
Dangerous living conditions in her house.
Degenerates the internal organs
Restricts strength for items she wants to open.

Are there people living in her attic, who at night
Come into her home and give her a terrible fright?
She thinks she has two identical homes,
Wants to be taken to the other one to be alone.

Medications to help her are questioned each day,
Thinking her husband is trying to poison her that way.
She sleeps during the day, awake at night.
Causing her husband a confusing sleeping blight.

But a recent move to a Memory Care Unit, Care Facility,
New approaches to redirect inappropriate behaviors they see,
Have worked for her, resulting in positive cooperation.
And my sister agreeing to be in groups instead of isolation.

Different medications are helping her relax, so she
Can enjoy sitting outside in the courtyard, you see.
Her pretty decorated room, bright, modern facility.
I'm far away, but blessed that is where she can be.

The positive, loving staff take excellent care of her each day
And communicate and send photos taken along the way.
If a loved one suffers from this disease, don't lose hope.
I pray you find effective ways to help you cope.

Dr. John Sayings:

Everybody wants to go to heaven, by and by.
But nobody wants to actually die.
The Sweet Ones die too early, you cry.
The Crotchety Ones seem to never die.

Having trouble bending over, your tennis shoe to tie?
Tennis shoes with Velcro, you should try.

Do you see a good dermatologist, Dr. John?
Only white people need to,
As dark-skinned races don't get skin cancer, Ron.

How long do you think I will live? Ron asked me.
I replied, Don't be selfish, you see.
If you are going to die,
Do so before your wife turns seventy-five.
If you wait until she's eighty,
Only reason a man would want your wife would be:
For her purse,
Or for a nurse.

A patient asked to be cleared to have sex that night, age 103.
I can not even clear you for a haircut, can't you see.

The Diabetic nerve pain you feel
Live with it. Learn to deal!

Your wife should be paid *over time pence*
For your high maintenance.

Ron, you are like a poodle dog indeed,
Grooming sessions, petting, massages you need.

Dr. John is my husband's internist. His medical expertise has successfully helped Ron's many challenges. Fifteen medications are prescribed for heart, lung, kidney, gout, blood pressure, circulatory, acid reflux, and diabetic issues. Dr. John's quick wit and humor, help keep every office visit relaxed and bearable.

Fantasy Football

*

I thought Fantasy Football was supposed to be fun.
But my dear husband stresses over
A missed touch down and intercepted run.

Injured players taken out of the game,
Then high-scoring points gone, insane.

Creating a roster, which players to pick?
The low scorers play, the high scorers get sick.

Training session to help get started,
Star players injured, off the field get carted.

Training session to help understand
How to choose a player with a good throwing hand.

Just when your team's winning,
Something unexpected happens—are you kidding.

Your best player is taken out.
No points for you tonight—time to pout.

So, I ask, what is a wife to do?
Stay in the kitchen and make chili or stew.

2020

Connect the Dots

Connect the dots, one, two, three.
What will the puzzle picture be?
As a child, a fun game.
As an adult, a new friend's name.

The dots appear when you first meet.
More dots added each time you greet.
Over the years, the dots accumulate.
Your mind will speculate.
Your imagination, stimulate.
Connecting the dots, we await
To see what formulates.

What will the puzzle picture be?
Connect the dots, one, two, three.
As a child, a fun game.
As an adult, your friend's acclaim.
As an adult, your friend's frame.
As an adult, what your friend overcame.
As an adult, your friend's fame to proclaim.

Limber Lynn

All the way from Cape Cod, Heritage Oaks scored a win,
Offering to lead yoga classes by a Limber Lady named Lynn.

Stressful times, fitness center closed due to quarantine.
We still needed to work out, despite COVID-19.

Lynn brought her inspiration, block, and strap,
Helped us get a better twist and wrap.

She helped our hips open up by sitting on our block.
We never minded longer class, not watching the clock.

Starting class with deep breaths and plenty of stretching,
Back, neck, side body, chest, arms reaching.

From Warrior II, straight into a Triangle Pose,
Easier way to open chest, hand toward toes.

Holding our Plank for longer breathing,
Various Down Dog positioning.

Her praise, excitement, clapping, and encouragement
Help us try harder for poses and our bodies in different ways bent.

We hope our tushes get smaller, our Angel Wings larger,
Our bodies more toned, our wings stronger.

And in meditation and relaxation, as we breathe in pink,
Of you, Lynn, we will continue to think.

Thank you for being an indispensable part,
Of us staying healthy, body, mind, attitude, heart.

Brenda F., Brenda S., Karen, Donna, Pat,
Basia, and Linda May 2020

Where Have All
My Poems Gone?

Where have all my poems gone?
Long time passing.
Where have all my poems gone?
Long time ago.
Where have all my poems gone?

Gone to greeting cards sent for special days.
Gone to school files given away.

Gone to original mailed without a copy made.
Gone to the scraps of paper I never saved.

Gone to bulletin board captions thrown away.
Gone to posters made, recycled to use another day.

Gone to old typewriters without a save button
Gone to old computers every one.

When will I ever learn?
When will I ever learn?

Friends

Accepting
    Including
        Know my name
            Glad I came
Like family
    They are family
        Loving
            Caring
                Giving
                    Generous
Ups, Downs
    Happiness, Frowns
        Always there
            When Where
                Kindhearted
                    Listening Resorted
Active lifestyles
    Bring smiles
        Healthy choices
            Inquisitive voices
            Learning
                Engaging
Surprises
    Birthday treats and wishes
        Get-well meal dishes
            Homemade masks
                COVID-19 task

Trustworthy True
   My best interest, too
      Desire to please God above
         I'm a recipient of their Love

Friends Called

Friends called for advice and help over the years,
Not because my life was perfect, but had fears.
They knew I survived difficult times,
When there were no reasons nor rhymes.

Ron had cancer, quintuple heart bypass surgery,
Lung, kidney, vascular difficulties.
Then heart valves replaced at the Cleveland Clinic.
How does one live when the spouse is so sick?

As a child, Jill broke her leg in the growth plate bone.
Would her leg be short or grow long?
Jen went through five years of fertility treatments,
Losing babies until dreams seemed lost and bent.

Moving many times with my husband's career
Starting over, missing those who were dear.
Miles away from friends and family.
Replacing school, church, doctors, quick as could be.
Marriage issues, rehab needed.
Counseling sessions, advice heeded.

My husband and I and our daughters are survivors!
Regardless of life challenges and chores.
We didn't know or like what often came our way.
We didn't know what we would have to say.

Friends call because they know I've been there
I will understand and help them dare
To trust in healing and staying the course.
Listening, encouraging, friendly force.

Thankfully we have our faith and hope.
Prayers bring strength, help us cope.
The trials brought trust and God's faithfulness stories.
That helped us pass on God's goodness and glory.
June, 2020

Books for Baby

Must be the teacher in me
Wants you to be smart as can be.

Enjoy this *A B C Book*.
Have fun taking a look.

Time spent reading with Mom and Dad
Will always make all very glad.

My daughters always wanted me to read
I Love You to the Moon and Back, indeed.

Saying those words as I turned out the light
Kissing them both good night.

May you enjoy two of my favorite books.
Over the years have fun taking lots of looks.

My dear friend Karen raised four sons, had three weddings and now, three daughters by marriage. But becoming a grandmother for the first time with a lifelong membership in the Grandparents Club, incredible. Books were sent for Riley's baby shower.

Sympathy Threads

Create my Tapestry

Moving away
I'm seldom there,
When friends lose a loved one
And are in despair.

I want them to know
Time also stopped for me.
Tears were shed,
Prayers spoken from bended knee.

A poem written
That took thought and time,
To send sympathy, hope, and love
Through my rhyme.

Mother

Mother, The more I learn about you,
The more I respect you,
The more I clearly see you, too.

I read between the lines and see,
The sacrifice and pain,
The hard work and rain,
The hope and love and joy,
Meaningful lives of each girl and boy.

I see through the layers that go back in time
And how those layers made you tick and rhyme.

Mother, the more I learn about you,
The more I will miss you
But will carry forward your memory and traditions, too.

In Memory of
George Auble

Kay, your warm smile, sparkling eyes, lovely face,
If time permits, we'd meet for an embrace.
I'd let you pour out your heart
Of little things from the start,
That touched you, lingered in your mind,
Now into your heart their way did find.

Bits and pieces from here and there,
Of memories you now want to share.
Memories to warm you when you feel alone,
Or uncertain of the unknown.
Memories to pass along to store,
So others can feel they know him more.

Father so special—
May you find comfort in the memories you shared,
And of yourself and your love to him you bared.

Friends for support—
May you find rest in their help and love,
Especially provided by God above.

God, your Heavenly Father, your sufficiency—
May you find peace in knowing He's been there
And is with you everywhere.
That your father is in a better place
Heavenly time, eternal space.
February 19, 1987

Kay, my special Indianapolis friend, shared church, Bible Study Fellowship, and four years of wonderful family life memories. Kay wrote and sang a song for me before I moved to California. Years later when her father died and I could not be there, I wrote this poem.

Oh Daughter Dear, Precious and Small

I'll give you everything, give you my all!
Cradling you in my arms,
I'll protect you from all harms.
Watching you grow and do your firsts,
Hope nothing will your balloons burst.
Such playfulness and joys.
Dolls and books and toys.
Sisters and friends and family,
So happy, what else could there be.
School and teachers and learning more.
Doors close but doors open for what life has in store.

Oh daughter dear, so precious but no longer small.
I will still give you everything, give you my all.
Father, mother, sisters, family.
Who could this man now in your life be?
New life adventuress for both you and me,
But far removed, how will I see?
The troubles of life bear down
Causing that drowning sound.
Is it good? Is it bad? Is it happy? Is it sad?
Will the good out weigh the bad?
Will the happy out weigh the sad?
No one knows the rhyme or reason.
Is there ever a good season?
Our screams and cries are not in vain
As we remember her name!
Her life and all she gave.
In our hearts we'll always save.

And for the life that could be,
Melissa chose now to be free!
We will continue to honor her memory.
And as in a moment her life was snapped.
We know in God's arms, Melissa is now wrapped.
So because Melissa goes to a better place,
We know we will one day see again her beautiful face.
Peace lies on the other side.
Hope for our broken hearts abides.
May 4, 1972 to October 15, 2016

Mayor Jack

I'll always remember my first exercise
class at Heritage Oaks, the HO,
When I walked into the Baptist church room, little did I know,
How inviting you would be as you came right up to me and said,
Hi, I am Eileen. Welcome, in your Christmas sweatshirt of red.

You were always bubbly, friendly, energetic, and caring,
And had fun stories you were always sharing.
I grew to respect and love you as a friend,
And enjoyed time together that we would spend.
Soon we learned that the tall man who walked by the house
Was Jack O'Flaherty, your spouse.

You were an endearing couple, an inspiration to all.
It was with much sadness I learned of his downfall.
I watched as you gently, lovingly helped your Jack,
And made sure he had nothing to lack.
You sacrificially loved him every way you could.
You cared for him as we knew you would.

We will always remember his big grim smile,
His long lanky legs, his gentlemanly style.
How he would watch and sit by the pool,
Your water aerobics class, looking so cool.
He always had something positive to say,
Anytime you spoke to him, on any day.

It is with sympathy, sadness, and tears
That we celebrate all of Jack's years.

Sadness for all you had to endure.
Sadness because there was no cure.
Comfort knowing of a better place.
Comfort knowing there is now a smile on his face.
Comfort knowing how many care,
Comfort knowing we want to be there.

Husband to Eileen, the love of his life, father to three sons and a daughter, Jack managed both the New York and then Tampa FBI offices. On his daily walks of short distance, Jack would be gone for hours, stopping to talk with everyone he passed. He never met a stranger. Everyone in the HO, Heritage Oaks, knew and loved him. He is deeply missed. 2016

Mother Dear

Mother Dear, I tried to love all parts of you,
The good, the bad, the ugly too.
The years rapidly tick by.
To make them rhyme and reason, we try.
Lives intertwined with difficult events in history.
Survival, moving, making your own family story.
Husband and children to love all your life.
Nurturing mother, attentive wife.

All the memories of our family.
All the things you tried to be.
The layers of life as we now look back in time
Unravel the stories that made us tick and rhyme.
All the moments in time we shared.
All the dreams we thought and dared.
Mother, the more I've learned about you
The more I respect and clearly see you, too.

My clothes may fade as time goes by,
But certain fun memories will never die.
I know you have a special angel up above
Watching over you forever with love.
You will now be with your husband through eternity
Just as you planned it would forever be.

Basia, may you find comfort in knowing we care.
And in your loss we want to share.

May fond memories bring joy to your heart, to your face a smile.
As you start your day by walking your mile
So here's to Vanda or Wanda, whatever her name
This world without her will never be the same.
October 4, 1923-July 26, 2019

A friend helped Basia's parents escape concentration camps in Poland and find a place to live Paris, France. This same friend later helped Basia's family move to America. Vanda was Basia's Mother's Polish name, which was changed to Wanda in the U.S. Wanda lived into her nineties. Caring for an aging, ill parent, living out of town, a challenging journey. For years, Basia lovingly, made that trip, created memories, and shared her mother's final hours.

Life's Layers
Through Time

Dearest Iris,
Marriage years add up to memories great,
Of Kenny, your dearly beloved, departed mate.

Our clothes may fade as time goes by,
But certain memories will never die.
As you look through the layers that go back in time,
To make sense of the reason or rhyme,

LOVE bound two souls together to face,
Life's hectic race and retirement's slower pace.
Work, studies, travels, interests, family,
Church, hobbies, all that life could possibly be.

And while there may be a deep sense of sadness,
We believe heaven is a glorious place of gladness.
So now, may fond memories comfort you,
And linger in heart and mind, too.

Know you have a special angel up above
Watching over you forever with *love*.
May you find comfort in knowing we care.
And are sharing in your loss and burden you bear.

My husband attended Fern Creek High School, where Iris was the
librarian. We keep in touch through Christmas letters. We participate
in the same Bible Study Fellowship in different cities. Iris liked to
compare notes about what we were studying.

In Memory of
Alvin Hyman

*Sixty-two years of marriage add up to memories great
Of your dearly beloved, departed mate.
Our clothes may fade as time goes by,
But certain memories will never die.*

*As you look through the layers that go back in time,
To make sense of the reason or rhyme.
Love bound two souls together to face,
Life's hectic race and retirement's slower pace.*

*From St. Louis to Heritage Oaks,
Al stayed active, making friends with many folks.
A special librarian with his big smile and unique looks,
Pushing that cart to organize the books.*

*His favorite line, I don't know what I do all day
But it takes me all day to do it (my way).
Memories of his jokes, funny sayings, and smiling face,
Brought happiness and laughter, no matter the day or place.*

*National Champs in Volleyball Senior Olympics.
He loved golf and the guys, with him over the years would stick.*

Work, travel, interests, theater plays, and family,
Hobbies, all that life could be.

And while there may be a deep sense of sadness,
We believe the end of illness and suffering brings gladness.
So now, may fond memories comfort you,
And linger in heart and mind, too.

May you find comfort in knowing we care.
And in your loss we want to share.

January 29, 2020

Deepest Sympathies

Agony and Pain!
Tears fall like heavy rain!
Such sadness, such madness.
Will any amount of time bring gladness?
Always helpful, never mean.
Now a victim of COVID-19.

Jeanne died Maundy Thursday, then Good
Friday's agony of the cross.
So many would feel such a great loss.
Praise God for Easter Sunday's Resurrection story.
Jeanne is in heaven seeing God's glory.

But death stops us in our tracks.
To assess our life and what it lacks.
Jeanne was ready, she leaves an inspirational legacy.
Her Christian life was one of service for all to see.

Daughter, Wife, Mother Dear,
Teacher, Counselor, Friend, always near.
Grandmother, far and wide your travels would take you.
To be with sons, daughter, and grandchildren, too.

We first met you, Waubonsie High School days,
You counseled and helped us in so many ways.
Moving from California to Naperville,
For my daughters, was no thrill.
Just Say No seminar, STEP parenting class,
Tough love compassion with a little sass.

I remember Howard opening the car door for you,
Encouraging boy friends to do the same, too

A perfect score on the ACT
Your son making you proud as could be.
Forgiveness lesson from a garage fire,
Teaching loving consequences her desire.

Helped Jill be accepted to Indiana University, IU,
Daughters Shelby and Taylor attend, Jill works there too.

Howard's new job, to Colorado he would go.
You lived with us, helped shovel snow.
But the time did come for you to drive cross-country.
Your car packed inside and on top, finally Howard to see.

Staying in touch over many past years
Through Christmas photos and letter cheers.
Your last letter full of special celebrations,
I will always cherish in memoriam.

My deepest sympathies to every family member.
Jeanne Tiffany's legacy will live on in you forever.

Love, Ron and Linda Potter

Jeanne's death was the first COVID-19 loss for me.
It was a devastating reminder of the seriousness of
that illness. I decided to share her legacy instead
of mourn her loss and gladly wear my mask.

April 9, 2020

Memories Dry
Our Teary Eyes

Renee,
As we are making memories,
We may not realize,
Those fun and happy memories
Will one day dry our teary eyes.

Our clothes may fade as time goes by,
But certain memories will never die.
In fact, the very person taken away,
May cause memories to grow dearer each day.

Mother, such a wonderful life, I'm tempted to say,
Why was your life taken away?
God calls us home in His own time
Even though we do not know the reason or rhyme.

God allows those memories to now comfort you
Every day in all that you do.
May you also find comfort in knowing we care
And in your loss we want to share.

Even though I did not know your Mother, I want to say
Deepest Sympathies are coming your way.

January, 2020

In Memory of Sweet Shirley Blanton

*Founding Member of Choral Singers
When St. John's Methodist first opened its doors.*

Years of marriage add up to memories great.
Of your dearly beloved, departed mate.
Our clothes may fade as time goes by.
But certain memories will never die.

As you look through the layers that go back in time,
To make sense of the reason or rhyme,
Love bound two souls together to face,
Life's hectic race and retirement's slower pace.

Work, studies, travels, interests, hobbies, family,
Church choir and all that life could possibly be.
And while there may be a deep sense of sadness,
We know heaven is a glorious place of gladness.

So now, may fond memories comfort you,
And linger in heart and mind, too.
Know you have a special angel up above
Watching over you forever with *love*.

May you find comfort in knowing we care,
And are sharing in your loss and burden you bear.

September 7, 1935—April 22, 2020

Shirley was married to Bob for sixty years and
taught second grade for forty-three years, almost
eighty-five years of loving service to many.

Jerry, Did You Know?

Your life was taken too suddenly.
Could this possibly be?
When you sang with the choir,
Praise to the Lord of the Small Broken Things,
It would be your last anthem before heavenly wings.

Jerry, did you know?
The tenor section will never be the same.
I'll miss looking for your music signed out by your name.
We thought you were a gentleman,
Always positive with a smile for certain.

Jerry, did you know?
The quarantine time you spent with your wife
Will become comforting memories of your life.
Your good friends were here
Helping Anita, whom you held so dear.

Jerry, did you know?
Your life will be remembered by friends and family
Because of the special ways you treated others daily.
The vacation trips you took with your wife,
Will be wonderful memories for the rest of her life.

Jerry, did you know?
Whatever amount of time on this earth is now gone,
It's our faith and love of God that lives on.
Our deepest sympathies to those left behind
We will miss you. You were one of a kind.

Jerald Edwin Laesser, seventy-six, a cancer survivor, was just returning home from a jaw reconstructive surgery. The following day, he unexpectedly passed away from a blood clot. September 16, 1943 –June 17, 2020.

Teaching School Threads

Create my Tapestry

As a child, I played school,
Others played house.
Cowboys and Indians were loud.
My students, quiet as a mouse.

Helped dance teachers with younger classes
Taught Red Cross Swim Lessons
Dealing with the masses.

Substitute teacher for many a year.
Classroom teacher, young lives to steer.

Always a Teacher

As a child, friends played cowboys, some played house,
I instead played school, my pupils quiet as a mouse.
I would set up my classroom with books and chalk board,
Assigned math problems, read stories, gave candy awards.
A teacher is what I always wanted to be.
In 1969, a teaching degree from Murray University.

First-grade teaching position at White Eagle School,
Loved teaching, would have been excited, as a rule.
But I taught sixth grade for several years,
Can first graders read, write, tie a shoe, my fears.
The journey was hard work but exciting.
My pupils, endearing, lovable, and inviting.

Then my Daughter joined our first-grade team,
We made newspaper headlines, it would seem.
We were first Mother-Daughter combo to
teach same school, same grade.
In our Indian Prairie School District, history we made.

We had the same last name.
Could you tell us apart, was that insane?
My jeans skirt was very long, a short jeans skirt she wore.
She had perfect vision, I needed colorful glasses galore.
However, I was in love with her student who,
Because of our last name, thought we were sisters, too.

When Jennifer later got married, her class came to the church.
When it was time, around the altar they would *perch*,
Singing their hearts out for all to hear,
A special song for their teacher dear.

Mandy the
Monkey Puppet

Taught sixth grade, now what to do?
I'm assigned to first graders who can't tie a shoe.
I need their attention, maybe a rhyme,
And a fun puppet to sponge up their time.

This is Mandy. She thinks she's pretty
dandy. She loves to eat candy.
She's in first grade and is very handy. Her
best friends are Sandy and Randy.
Welcome to first grade, where we learn to read, write, and say,
The ABC's and our one, two, threes.
Mandy's special, don't you see? She's a special friend to me.
She can't read, she can't talk. She can't fly, she can't walk.
But Mandy's a Math Wizard and later you'll see,
Just how smart she can really be.
There's a game she likes to play.
When you go home, she hides each day.
When you come each morning to school,
Don't forget the rule.
Walk into our room quiet as a mouse.
Look around our classroom house.
Put your Take Home Folder in the bin.
Do the Entrance Graph to begin.
Back packs on the back of your chair.
Sharpen your pencil, check your hair.
If you see where Mandy might be,
Go to your desk, begin a Journal entry.
Remember, quiet as a mouse.
After all this is Mandy's house.

405

In your journal write for me,
Where you think Mandy might be.
Why you think she's dandy,
What could you feed her? She likes candy.
Tell me about her friends Randy and Sandy.
How you think she's handy.
Write anything about your day.
Write anything you want to say.
We'll take turns sharing what we write.
Think about it at home tonight.
Have fun learning with Mandy each day.
She decides if you get extra play.
Smile, know Mandy likes you too.
Especially if you are new.

Flight

Daedalus and Icarus flew to the sun.
People thought the Ornithopter would be fun.

Montgolfier Balloon—up, up we go!
The Dirigible went very slow.

Lilienthal Glider needed air to get by.
The Wright Brothers' plane, first machine to fly.

Bleriot's monoplane first to fly across water.
People thought he was insane.
Madame de Larouche first woman to pilot a plane.

First pilot to cross the Atlantic, Lindbergh his name.
Amelia Earhart, the first woman to do the same.

The helicopter could fly straight up or down.
Yeager's X-1 flew faster than sound.

X-15 the first aircraft rocket.
Project Mercury, Shepard and Glenn first Americans in space yet.

Gemini Program, more space exploration and none too soon.
Apollo 11 first Man on the Moon!

Skylab, the first Space Station for working in space
Space Shuttle is reusable, rides piggyback
to return to a specific place.
The history of flight and how man learned to fly.
What kind of travel will come next for us in the sky?

When I taught first grade, we did a unit on Flight, with a *trip to the moon*. The children dressed-up in *space suits*, fashioned and sewed by the mothers. *Air packs*, made from cereal boxes covered in foil, were strapped to each *astronaut's* back. This poem, space photos, and the moon adventure helped the students learn the history of air and space travel. That first grade adventure was in the late nineties. As I type this poem into my computer, Space X Crew Dragon, took off for a nineteen-hour trip to the Space Station. Space travel has advanced beyond my comprehension. May 30, 2020.

Travel Threads

Create My Tapestry

Did we travel, take a vacation?
Moved instead to a new location.

Louisville, Kentucky; Minnetonka, Minnesota;
San Ramon, California; Indianapolis, Indiana.

Newbury Park, California; Naperville, Illinois;
Sarasota, Florida, retirement joy.

Did We Travel?

Travels did include four trips to Hawaii
Different islands, volcanoes, golf courses to see.

Our daughters enjoyed Disney World and Disneyland,
It's a Small World After All and beach sand.

Williamsburg, Virginia, and Washington, D.C.
Lincoln Memorial, money printed to see.

With my Mother's synchronized ice skating team,
China and Japan tours, exciting scenes.

Kentucky trips to visit friends and family.
Spring break, Florida sun for daughters to see,

Niagara Falls, Canadian and U.S. sides,
Daniel Island, South Carolina beach tides.

Paris, France; Hamburg, Germany; Netherlands,
Allianz golf competition in the German meadowlands.

Arc de Triomphe, Eiffel Tower, Notre Dame,
Cathedrals, Louvre, tulips, windmills, River Seine.

Weddings meant daughters moved away.
Visiting their states for a fun stay.

Memories made always timeless,
Time spent with grandchildren, priceless.

Mediterranean Cruise

Thursday; June 12, 2014; Rome, Italy
Our first cruise, a ten-night Mediterranean,
A Billion-dollar, nineteen-month-old ship, *Celebrity Reflection.*
We arrived, June 12, 2014 in Rome
Visiting Father Tommy, our neighbor's son from home.
Our hotel, wonderfully quiet Palazzo Cesi.
TV in Italian, tiny shower, a former monastery.
Lunch at Father Tommy's favorite, quaint as could be.
Ristochicco, with Lasagna, bread, wine, salad Caprese.

St. Peter's Square, Vatican City.
We already love Italy.
The Sistine Chapel Ceiling, with three hundred figures,
Was painted five centuries ago, on an area covering 2,500 meters.
Father Tommy's private tour: Pantheon, Roman Forum,
St. Paul Basilica, spectacular ceiling, cross door, Colosseum.
University Seminary, Father Tom oversees priests' training.
That night overheard male voices at Vespers praises claiming.
He took us behind the ropes, as the Pope goes.
St. Peter's Basilica with Pieta, Swiss guards he shows.
Good-bye busy Rome, traffic, crowded streets.
We'll miss the lighted dome at night and good eats.

Friday; June 13; Port Civitavecchia, Italy
Hello, Cruise ship. Port Civitavecchia, departure point.
We are moving out to sea. Full moon tonight.
Our cabin, number 2164, sofa, closet
storage, champagne, and fruit.
Connecting balconies for passengers, Rice, Gunder, Potter to boot.
The *three kings* watching as we leave port.

The *three queens* relaxing, our jewelry to sort.

Saturday; June 14; Messina, Sicily
Largest island in Mediterranean, volcanic
soil makes best wine in the world,
Yachts built in Palermo, Taormina black
rock beaches with waves swirled.
Unfortunately, Rick became ill, he and
Linda to our ship decided to go.
Alcantara Valley Gorge formed by forty miles Mount Etna lava flow.
Severe shortage, water used for people and crops, no pets.
Greek fortress highest point in town,
spectacular valley view, you bet.
Lemon, orange, olive groves in valley. Warm
African air currents each day
With volcanic soil, produce unique grape and fruit flavor array.
In different altitudes, different fruits and kinds of grapes grow.
Country ruled by Romans, Turks, Arabs, as architecture shows.
Smokin' Mount Etna, narrow streets,
gorgeous window flower boxes, snow.
Gambino Winery, seven wines to sample, as off to lunch we go.
The *Godfather* movie, filmed all over Sicily,
pieced together by director,
World War II German Pillbox (hid machine
guns), good-bye guided tour
Back to our ship, Table 236, delicious dining with Orville, our waiter.
Bands, singing, contests, competitions, casino, bars, for fun later.
Whitney Houston Tribute, Comedian, Musicals, Ventriloquist,
Cirque du Soleil acts, Dancing, fabulous nightly Entertainment.

Sunday; June 15; Sea Day
We relaxed in our private top-deck alcove,
with lunch and Ron napping.
Then the Hammocks, quiet covered solarium,
Linda swimming and lapping.

For dinner, a Tuscan Restaurant for our formal dining night.
Linda had her favorite chocolate mousse dessert delight.

Monday; June 16; Athens (Piraeus), Greece
Piraeus, Athens's main port in the Mediterranean Sea.
We watched docking into the port from our ship's balcony.
Fancy yachts, narrow streets, Olympic Stadium, bus tour,
Acropolis ruins, Parthenon, most recognizable in the world for sure.
Always in restoration
To prevent further deterioration.
Ron and Linda in their matching outfits of yellow and gray.
Quaint Plaka shopping, eternity symbol
bracelets, what a great day.

Tuesday; June 17; Ephesus (Kusadasi), Turkey
Good morning. Port city means *Bird Island.* Most attractive city
On the Aegean Sea, west coast of Turkey. Colonies began in 10 B.C.
Friends of Gunders joined us for the Sea Song Bus Tour to see
The Glories of Ephesus, very hot day, I recall, for us it would be.
The Glories of Ephesus established by Alexander the Great,
The ruins showed wall decorations and beautiful mosaics.

This advanced civilization had three-story
homes, central heating, fountains.
One of the Seven Wonders of the Ancient World, well maintained.
Ephesus was the center of culture, faith, and trade.
Many important world decisions right here were made.
Great Theater seated twenty-five thousand
spectators, for plays to see,
Gladiator fights and discussions on
religion, politics, and philosophy.

Visited House of the Virgin Mary where she
lived the last years of her life

After the resurrection, safe from Jewish
persecution and a life of strife.
Statue of Mary, Hope Prayer Wall,
Lunch at a Turkish restaurant with plenty of food for all.
John, the beloved disciple, brought Mary here.
Wrote his Gospel and letters in the Bible and is buried near.
The small chapel built over St. John's grave later gave way
To a huge Basilica, impressive ruins remain today.
Farewell, Turkey. Thank you to the Gunder's special friends,
Arranged the tour, helped cook lunch, ice
cream treats, day's perfect end.
Back on the ship, relaxation nap time for
Ron, for Linda a swim it would be.
Delicious dinner, a Violinist who performed for the Royal family.

Wednesday; June 18; Rhodes, Greece
Largest of the Dodecanese Islands, sunshine
three hundred days of the year
Twenty miles from Athens, Greece, so the mainland is near.
Medieval walled city, ancient acropolis, not small.
Shopping streets form a maze inside the high walls.
This citadel, built by (the Order of Knights
of St. John) the Hospitallers.
One of the best European medieval towns preserved.
Jewelry for Linda, necklace, bracelet, earrings would be.
Spectacular beaches, wading to cool off in the Aegean Sea.

Thursday; June 19; Santorini, Greece
Boats to tender us to shore and back,
Five hundred eighty-eight steps up cliff side
zigzag pathway, can one hack?
Cable Car line option or mule ride to the cliff top.
Relaxed atmosphere, colorful flowers, please, time, just stop.
Small, circular archipelago of volcanic
islands in the South Aegean Sea.

Many come to uncover the Lost City of Atlantis mystery.
One hundred twenty-five miles from the Greece mainland,
The view from atop the island, spectacularly grand.
Santorini is white-lime-washed villages clinging to the volcanic cliffs.
Black-sand beaches, crystal-clear blue water, boats adrift
Attract visitors, make this island a wonder to behold.
Mamma Mia, not just filmed here, but on
other islands, we were told.

Friday; June 20; Mykonos, Greece
In the deep blue waters of the Mediterranean Sea,
Lies one of the most interesting places in all of Greece to be.
Quaint cobblestone streets, beautiful
landscapes, countless bays, beaches.
Hundreds of little churches, windmills,
picturesque white painted villages.
History of the island inhabited by Cretes, Egyptians,
Romans, Franks, Turks, and Venetians.
A fun way to travel, we rented four-wheelers to explore,
Golden sandy beaches with bars for drinks, food, and more.
Relaxing with the wind in my hair, in my toes, sand.
Sunshine on my shoulder, as far as I can see, blue, blue ocean.

Saturday; June 21; Sea Day
Last chance to relax, enjoy all amenities of our ship.
Don't want an end to this Mediterranean Cruise trip.
Another gourmet dinner, excellent entertainment.
The service, superb, a definite asset.

Sunday; June 22; Naples, Italy
Most European towns close stores on Sunday.
What are our options for our last cruise day?
Let's see Naples via the On-Off Bus.
Medieval fortress, government buildings, hotels, a must.

Lots of scooters and traffic, no available parking.
People out walking, talking, relaxing.
Homes, downtown area, port, market shops, cathedrals.
Goodbye, Naples. Final dinner, Top Deck 15, Lawn Club Grill.
Nine-person serving staff, grilled Lamb Chops,
Delicious shrimp, steaks, scallops.
For dessert, Chocolate-Chip Cookie baked in a small dish,
Topped with ice cream and to return to
cruising, our dream and wish.

Monday; June 23; Rome Airport, Home

Royal Caribbean Cruise

Sunday, Cruise Day one.
Get ready for fun in the sun!
We boarded the amazing *Allure of the Seas*,
An enormous cruise ship with every amenity!

Rock climbing wall, shops, entertainment, food snacks,
Ice cream, desserts, music, relaxing with drinks and time to unpack.
First night, first dinner in the main dining hall.
Oh no, a robbery to jar us all!

Stolen jewelry made Linda G. very sad.
Stolen jewelry made all of us mad.
Entertainment was Aqua Theater's *Ocean Aria*
High-diving stunts and plenty of splashing to thrill all.

Monday, Cruise Day two
Nassau, Bahamas, with shops and buildings that were not very new.
Sushi for appetizers at Izumi.
Rick bought the entire bottle of Sake.

Professional ice show with acrobatic dancing,
Cute costumes, excellent skating, kept everyone clapping.
Dinner was remembered because Linda P. had three desserts.
I bet her tummy really did hurt.

So hilariously funny was the Comedy Club skit.
We laughed so hard our sides almost split.
With lines like *Son, do not marry that black girl.*
Don't worry Dad, I won't marry any girl.

Tuesday, Cruise Day three
Breakfast at Solarium peaceful as can be.
Watches purchased, kids parade fun.
Rices, Ron, and Rick relaxed in the sun.

Entertaining lunch at Johnny Rockets,
With Linda dancing, thinking she was a Rockette.
Rum in their milk shakes added to the day,
Ron and Rick drinking in the morning, what can I say?

The Mamma Mia play brought tears to our eyes
As we watched the young performing girls and guys.
Familiar songs from the movie past
Rejuvenated memories to last.

Delicious Italian dinner for our night fling,
Lasagna, shrimp, Tiramisu, and bread pudding.

Wednesday, Cruise Day four on Allure of the Seas
Boat trip excursion, how difficult could that be?
Cabby dropped us at the wrong location
But thankfully we were rescued and got on with our excursion.

St. Thomas, Virgin Islands, Velocity Boat trip.
The captain let us snorkel and get a cool dip
Snorkeled by turtles, coral, and fish.
At Joe's Rum Hut had lunch, which was a delicious dish.

Beautiful homes nestled in the hillsides to see.
Private islands, beaches, and homes of Reggie Jackson, Donna
Summers,
Rockefeller, and Kenny Chesney.

An elaborate *Seventies Disco Inferno Street Parade*
Took place on Deck 5, the Royal Promenade.

While the men had Casino action that night,
The ladies watched a movie and enjoyed the night lights.

Thursday, Cruise Day five
Off to explore Saint Kitts and have some jive.
Our version of *Wild Hogs*
With Rick, Ron, and Larry Dog.

150 CC Scooters did the trick.
We saw the island volcano, beaches, and scenery, thanks to Rick.
Lunch and shopping at Reggae Beach Bar,
Then back on our bikes, who needs a car?

How strange to be driving on the wrong side of the street.
Luckily a nice breeze took care of the heat.
Good-bye mongoose, monkeys, beautiful aqua water.
Hello, Chop House, for a specialty dinner.

Earl Turner entertained us with a *sing-along*
Of oldies and goodies tunes and songs.
He had the audience engaged
And we sang and clapped and moved enraged.

Friday, Cruise Day six
So many activities from which to pick,
Breakfast at the Wipe Out Cafe,
Looks like a workout and massage day.

Lunch at Giovanni's Table, delicious and swell.
As luck would have it, the ship's captain was eating there as well.
Relaxing on deck in the afternoon.
Our trip time is ending all too soon.

Music Trivia, Name the Tune and Artist
We had fun scoring ten out of fifteen points on our list.
Final night in the main dining room.
Delicious four-course meals and great service ending all too soon.
Late-night walking on the ship's top deck,
Refreshing breeze, could see the moon with a tilt of our neck.

Saturday, Cruise Day seven
This week has been heaven.
Exercising, then donuts and coffee at Starbucks.
Johnny Rockets serves breakfast, good for our luck.

Seeing very calm, blue waters, relaxing on deck 15.
It's the first time another vessel has been seen.

In the Amber Theater, we enjoyed the *Blue Planet* show,
Really going to miss this nightly entertainment when home we go.
A tree whose trunk and branches
Come alive with acrobatic dances.
A curtain that makes the stage look like the ocean deep
With jellyfish and marine life dancers that swim and leap.

Giovanni's Table where we decided to eat
Gave most of our taste buds a *send off to home* treat,
Stuffed Shrimp, lasagna, Eggplant Parmesan,
Tiramisu, and Crab Ravioli.
Thank you for the wonderful dinner, Giovanni.

And as our cruise comes to an end,
We are most grateful for the love of good friends.
The Cruising Six have done it again.
And I'm so glad we all came.

What a wonderful way to celebrate.
It has been one long, extended date.
Thank you to all who made the plans.
Good luck getting to the airport in your van.

Safe travels to one and all.
God bless until we meet again to have a ball.

This cruise was a Fortieth Anniversary celebration for dear friends Dianne and Larry Rice. Dianne's sister Linda and husband Rick also went. We called ourselves the *Cruising Six*. Our first adventure had been a fourteen-day Mediterranean Cruise.

World War II Museum, New Orleans

∅

Day one; Tuesday; March 3, 2020
Our Southwest flight, extra thirty minutes to circle city due to fog
Then a shuttle to Best Western, St.
Christopher Hotel, recorded in our log.
Lunch at Creole House, Linda ordered Shrimp
and Grits with Gouda Cheese.
Ron chose Poached Eggs on Crawfish Cakes, please.
VIP Bus Tour, guided information on:
Cafe Du Monde, City Park, our very first Beignet.
Powdered sugar all over my black pants and face.
French Quarters, every street will change its name,
French and Americans couldn't agree on street names.
City Park, **a** 1,300-acre oasis, lakes, roller-
coaster, sports fields for events,
Disney life-size figures, amusement parks, trails, and bikes for rent.
Cemeteries with graves entombed above ground, flowers budding.
Seventeenth Street Canal, during Katrina,
caused destruction and flooding.
Lake Pontchartrain, 630 square miles of
brackish estuary, forty miles long,
Is the second largest inland salt water body in the United States.
The Causeway Bridge is twenty-four miles in length.
Garden District, Antebellum historic
mansions built before the Civil War.
St. Louis Cathedral, triple steeples, in North
America the oldest cathedral.
Dinner at Oceana Cafe, French Quarters, Crab Cakes with slaw.
Pappy had Seafood Platter with Oysters
on Half Shell and ate it all.

Day two and Day three; Wednesday and Thursday; March 4–5
World War II Museum, spent two whole days
Immersed in reliving the horrors of World War II ways.
Stained Glass Exhibit; Shards of glass collected from bombed
churches destroyed stained glass windows, by a chaplain
who insisted on going to Europe for service and searches.
(This Chaplain was too young to enlist,
Finally to European front lines was sent on his insist.)
Glass sent to the United states, artistically
redesigned into artwork reflecting the light
Of freedom and future peace at the end of the fight.
Warehouse Wall shows World Map with simultaneous expansion,
Hitler in Europe, Japan in Southeast Asia,
country by country invasion!
Into Hitler and Japanese harm's way,
Old films showed battles, bombings each day.
Venues where bombs caused your seat to rock,
Snow falling on audiences as on movie screen, mock.
From 1937 to 1940, Japan invades Korea, Formosa, Vietnam, China,
Midway, Marshall Islands, Dutch West
Indies, Guam, Thailand, Burma.
Germany invades North Africa, Italy, Sicily,
Austria, Poland, Netherlands,
Norway, Switzerland, Belgium, Russia, England, France, Finland.
1941; Attack on Pearl Harbor, Japan declares
war on the United States.
1942; Germany also declares war on the United States.
One feels the anguish, the greed of power, the horror of lost life,
Stories, accounts, films of actual battles,
no more husband, child, wife.
We listened to many audio accounts of heroes sent
Into years of battles, their lives spent.

1942; The United States joins forces with allies to fight back.
Still years of battles, heroes emerge, plans for major attacks.

1942–1945; United States wins Battle of Midway, Guadalcanal,
other sea battles, and Iwo Jima, Okinawa. The *Final fall of Japan!*
The United States wins back North Africa,
Sicily, Italy, France, and Normandy,
Battle of the Bulge, other countries. *Final fall of Germany!*
Saw models of USS Arizona, sank at Pearl Harbor, horrific day,
USS Missouri; Location for Japan signing
surrender, September 2, 1945, Tokyo Bay.
The Museum is a meticulous, masterful, marvel.
Each day an emotionally exhausting journey travel,
Experiencing the War, invasion progression, from beginning to end.
God won over Evil, the world could now mend.

You can manufacture weapons and purchase ammunition any time.
But you cannot buy valor nor pull heroes off an assembly line.

Day four; Friday; March 6, 2020
Our three-day, adventure trip to New Orleans, has come to an end.
Time to return home and share with our friends.
Everyone should experience the *World War II Museum,*
To gain appreciation for our costly freedom.
Many sacrificed so much, both day and night,
So freedom's light and future peace could
shine at the end of the fight.

To family members, thank you for your service.
My father, Irvin Messel, served in the Army
Air Corps during World War II.
My Uncle, Robert Jandt, also served in World War II.
My husband, Ronald Potter, served in the
Army during the Vietnam War.
My nephew, Major Driskell, has served, as
a Marine, for the past 23 years.

Tribute Threads

Create My Tapestry

My poem, the statement, my gift
For helping and giving others a lift.

To show gratitude for the beauty
Above and Beyond the Call of Duty.

To show respect for going the extra mile,
Always with energy, love, and a big smile.

To show admiration for your person,
Who cannot be replaced, that's for certain.

Sallie Mae Teacher Award

Jefferson County Schools, Louisville, Kentucky,
A State-level Representative presents for Elementary,

The Sallie Mae First Class Teacher Award
Given to a first-year teacher whose class was impossibly hard.

A class of students, challenging issues to overcome,
Insurmountable struggles these young students came from.

Emotional, psychological, learning disabilities
Home life, family dysfunction, financial difficulties.

A teacher in this environment suddenly has to be
Creative, compassionate, competent, you see,

Poverty at home, little food to eat
Awareness at school, best way to help, a treat.

Free breakfast, free lunch, fluoride treatment to start the day.
The teacher has to be all and do all in every way.

How does a young, inexperienced, first-year teacher survive?
Loving, caring, determined for each student to thrive.

This award based on superior instructional skills each day
Interaction with students, faculty, and parents, come what may.

And so we honor Miss Jennifer Renee Potter
Who has proven she is a genuine teacher.

Miss Jennifer Renee Potter taught at
Trunnell Elementary School
7609 St. Andrews Church Road
Louisville, Kentucky
June 1996

Daughters of All Ages

Mother-Daughter Banquet

Here's to you, Daughters of all ages
Each of you at different stages.
There are those daughters who,
Are experiencing life fresh and new.

Baby daughter, such a wonderful joy,
Even if you were expecting a boy.
Remember the fun, choosing a name,
If only Mom and Dad agree on the same.
And every single thing they do,
A first for them, a first for you.
First word, first smile, first tooth, first step.
Remember photos and notes you kept.
Daughters are sugar, spice, everything nice.
Did the nurse just check for lice?
What a cutie in your dress and hat.
Soon replaced with a softball and bat.

What memories of babies you've known,
Daughter, granddaughter, yourself, warm you when alone?

Wonderful stage, wonderful time.
We move to rocking horse and rhyme.

(Jill asked), Was I a Terrible Two? (Jen
asked), Was I a Trusting Three?
Yes. Yes. And I remember your first skinned knee.
(Jill asked), Was I a Frustrating Four and Fascinating Five?

How did I stay sane and alive?
You spent your days playing, running about.
Never got tired. Just wore me out.
You were six, in school all day.
I had to let go, let you go your own way.
Your sister had no one with whom to play.
Chicken pox, mumps, coughs, sneezes,
Colds, cuts, childhood diseases.
Broken bones, plenty of plaster.
Band-Aids and pills to make you heal faster

Those elementary years were fun,
A time of trying new things for everyone.
Were yours, School days, school days.
Dear ole Golden Rule days.
Reading and writing and arithmetic.
Taught to the tune of a hickory stick?
Or were they, School days, school days.
Can't wait for computer lab days.
Speed reading, cursive writing, new modern math.
No TV games if we provoke the teacher's wrath.
Projects, homework, reports galore.
Games spread all over the floor.
Jump rope, paper dolls, cards, and jacks,
Hide and Seek, Red Light, Mom, your life lacks.

Soccer, softball, did you try a sport?
Swimming, skating, building a fort?
Gymnastics and dancing to develop the body.
Health food and vitamins. Is that how you saw me?
I just wanted you to have every opportunity,
To see what choices you could be.
That's why I encouraged piano and singing,
Cello and Bell Choir, my ears are still ringing.
I had visions of you dancing on a stage,

Or going to Washington, becoming a page.
Being in the Olympics, hopes for you.
Who knows what dreams may someday come true?

What memories do you have of childhoods you've known,
Your daughter, granddaughter, yourself, that warm you when alone?

Wonderful stage. Wonderful time.
We move to teen years and sick joke rhymes.
So here's to you, Daughters of all ages
Each of you at different stages.

Remember the day you turned thirteen years and said,
Hooray! I'm a teen. Your mom said, Oh, dread.
I had my first date, my first long dress,
Your father pretended he was handling the stress.
Boyfriends, girlfriends, parties, and fun.
Vacation trips, days in the sun.
Clubs, activities, Friday night ball games.
Do you remember high school teachers' names?
Do you remember your teen years hair do?
Did you rat, roll, weave, or perm it, too?
Did you brush, pick, iron, flatten, or crimp?
Did you use mousse, gel, hair spray, tease so it wouldn't go limp?
Did you boogie, ballroom, jitterbug, or twist?
If there was a sock hop, would you have missed?
Did you do the Big Apple and Truck on Through?
Love Elvis, the Beatles, the Beastie Boys, too?
Did you drive your Mom crazy with making noise,
Phone calls, and dates with strange-looking boys?

Do you remember who taught you a car to drive,
And how your Mom prayed you'd remain alive?
Dissecting a frog or chemistry lab,
In makeup, did you like to dab?

High School memories whether present or past,
Will always linger in your heart to last.
Graduation Day finally came,
You knew you'd just never be the same.
Hopes, plans, so much to do.
Prayers your dreams would come true.
I cut the apron string. You flew away.
But your memories would always stay.

All the prayers to cover the worries.
All the fears, hopes, and hurries.
Suddenly, everything was worthwhile,
Seeing you as an adult, no longer a child.
The dolls, buggies, games put away,
You were off to college to stay.
You had a job, a career of your own.
Now your Pooh Bear was all alone.

What memories do you have of teens you've known
Your daughter, granddaughter, yourself, that warm you when alone?

Wonderful stage. Wonderful time.
We move to men and love-letter rhymes.
So here's to you, Daughters of all ages,
Each of you at different stages.

You knew by the twinkle in her eye,
That this was no ordinary guy.
Just a feeling, you didn't have to say,
Knew she'd brought this man, home to stay.
Whatever the plans, whatever the reason,
Whatever the place, whatever the season.
Floating down the aisle, in that white gown,
You were the proudest Mom around.
All the prayers to cover the worries.

All the fears, hopes, and hurries.
Suddenly, everything was worthwhile,
Seeing your daughter walk down that aisle.

Then your life took a brand-new twist.
New memories were added to your list.
You and your husband were unexpectedly alone.
The house seemed so empty with no one at home.
And little by little, you began to
Enjoy it being just he and you.
As your daughter lives out her life,
You relive memories of being a wife.

What memories do you have of adults you've known,
Mother, grandmother, yourself, that warm you when alone?

Wonderful stage. Wonderful time.
From adulthood to Golden Anniversary rhyme.
So we honor you Daughters of all ages,
Who have survived all of your stages.

We pause now to remember, daughters not here,
That we hold in our hearts most dear.
Father, you have the vision. You have the plan.
You hold each one of us in your hand.
We thank you, Dear Lord, for all of life's stages.
And each of the *Daughters of all ages.*

For a Mother-Daughter Banquet, my two
daughters and I read this poem.
Jill, in elementary school, read her corresponding part. Jennifer, in
middle school, read her appropriate lines. I read the *mother* lines.

435

Tribute to Ava

'Twas the night of PTA elections and all through our house
The coffee odor was perking as well as our mouse.
The notes had been sent to the members with care,
In hopes that a large number soon would be there,

Rather than nestled all snug in their beds,
While visions of pleasurable plans vanished from their heads.
Jim in his suit and Nan in her bauble,
Had just settled their brains with their usual prattle.

When out of the group amid all our chatter,
Came Ava's soft voice, asking how she could matter.
The group immediately moved like a flash,
Tore on their coats and went out the door with a dash.

The competent gleam of our new chosen president
Gave the luster we needed to end the event.
And now that the end of her term is near,
We hold appreciation for her guidance this year.

What a conscientious delight, so lively and quick.
Our thanks to you for sharing her, Nick.
More rapid than eagles the projects they came.
Ava phoned, organized, and thanked us by name.

Now Registration, now Meetings, now Faire and Appreciation.
On Newsletter, on Fundraisers, on Spotlight and Reflection.
To the top for our school, to the top of our county.
Let our energies and efforts be our bounty.

As dry leaves that before the wild hurricane fly,
When Ava meets with an obstacle, away the problems die.
So up to the school the volunteers they flew,
With cars full of helpers and Ava, too!

And then in a twinkling, Flo heard from the roof
The prancing and pawing of each volunteer hoof.
As she drew in her hand and was turning around,
Down the hallway they came with a bound.

Ava was dressed all in Jag, from her head to her foot,
Her clothes by this time were all tarnished with mimeograph soot.
A bundle of papers she had carried in hand,
And she looked like a Fashion Model well in command.

Her eyes, how they twinkled, her hair fashionably curly,
Her looks so classy, even when you saw her so early.
Her mouth was like Brett's, drawn up like a bow,
Her Great Pyrenees were as white as the snow.

A cute little giggle and a flash of her teeth,
An aura of exotic beauty encircled her like a wreath.
Her Nick's the one with beard and little round belly,
That shook when he laughed like a bowlful of jelly.

A wink of Ava's eye and a twist of her head,
Soon gave one to know they had nothing to dread.
She spoke few words but went straight to her work,
And filled all the positions, but used not a jerk.

And risking her acrylics, despite the task,
And giving a smile, no matter what asked,
She sprang to the challenge, to her board gave a whistle,
And away her term flew like the down of a thistle.

But I heard her exclaim, ere she drove out of sight,
Best wishes to all, and to all a good night.

Ava was President of the Parent Teacher Association
at Newbury Park High School, Newbury Park, California in
the 1980's. I was asked to write a poem to the rhythm
of the famous, *'Twas the Night Before Christmas.*

Remembering Pastor Lawson

Received a letter just the other day.
When you move, mail's exciting in a way.
This letter from Westlake Church, California, caught my eye.
As I read the letter, I said, *Oh my.*
I knew it was coming, you guess what's in store.
Hard to accept someone opening a new door.
As each family member arrived home that day,
They responded in turn, the following way:

Jill said, "Pastor Lawson worked hard, he deserves a break.
There is nothing he won't do or try to make.
Proud of our success in Confirmation class.
He wanted us to learn lessons that would last.
No wonder we've been searching, but can't find
A church family like we left behind.
It's not the same when Pastor's not there
To give the sermon and pray the prayer.
All will miss him because he is so dear.
Have to treasure memories of each year."

Jenny said, "Wish we could be there a day
Before Pastor leaves for retirement way.
I'd give him a hug and say I love you.
Sorry my Confirmation Class bugged you.
Moving to California, you were there each day,
Saying, I know it's hard to make your way.
Come to Youth Group and Confirmation Class.
You'll make friendships and memories to last.

You were right, it all fell into place.
Church, the difference, smiles on my face.
Struggled with death, my grandpa and two friends.
Your counsel and prayers brought healing amends."

Ron said, "His support, advice on EMC.
His confidence in what I could be.
Praise, encouragement, each step of the way.
Always kind, helpful, loving words to say.

When we moved to the city that's breezy,
He said, 'Doing what's best is not easy.'
He knows people, a man of insight,
Helping others brings him great delight."

Linda said, "Visiting before Lent,
Never forgotten the letter he sent.
Pastor's example of a godly life,
Loving, forgiving, regardless of strife.
Sermons without notes, Homiletics, clear.
Easy applications with stories dear.
His prayers and desires for the world's hungry.
Taking care of the least, never greedy.
Attending all Sunday School openings
With the children for prayers and singing.
Marvelous memory, each member's name.
Reminds me that Jesus knows the same.
You've influenced us in many ways.
Excited to see harvest in later days."

Joyce, your constant support, wife's loyalty.
Friendly word and smile for all to see.
Your loving and kind and gentle way,
Each day of the week, not just on Sunday.

New members' open house generosity
Fellowship, refreshments, hospitality.
Thousands of requests through the prayer chain.
Strength through answered prayers for all to gain.
Your varied roles in the women's groups for service and study.
Fun at the Sunday, Mother-Daughter Tea.
Care for mother Mildred, in your home here.
Her presence each Sunday, special and dear.
Behind a great man, a great woman stands.
We've seen you be Pastor's right and left hands.
We know from Scripture, God has a plan
For each Godly woman, Godly man.
God has spoken. Pastor heeded the call.
You, your family, will be missed by all.
A mixture of sadness and of joy.
You begin a new chapter of employ.
We love you. God bless you on your way.
God's peace and joy each and every day.
As Always, Ron, Linda, Jennifer, and Jill Potter.
September 3, 1989

STEP Class

&

We came with questions and fears
Of how to deal with those teenage years.
Some of us angry, some confused,
Some befuddled, some bemused.

She said, *Step right up, step right this way
For a Systematic Training for Effective Parenting today.*

*Step one; Goals of Teen Misbehavior now etched in my brain:
Attention, power, revenge, inadequacy,
excitement, peer acceptance to gain.
Never give attention on demand.
Bow out of power struggles as quickly as you can.
Win cooperation by enlisting help, opinions,
suggestions from the teen.
They'll see mutual respect, trust, and not say, You're mean.*

*Step two; Your family constellation should be kept in mind,
It determines how each member will shine.
Family atmosphere can be encouraging,
If independence, respect, acceptance,
equality, consistency we bring.*

*Step three; Life's an adventure, not a test.
You can't fail parenthood. Just do your best.
When dealing with the emotions of your teen,
Do the unexpected, watch nonverbal behavior,
use humor, don't be mean.*

Step four; Discouragement is the basis for most teen failures.
Parents' major role is to be an encourager.
Instead of saying, You weren't ready for the match today.
Say, Noticed game, faster and stronger than last I saw you play.
Do encourage, but don't praise,
As your teen will fear failure of new ways.
Do nothing for your teens they for themselves can do.
Pampering your teen will not help him build
confidence and self-reliance, too.

Step five; Ask who owns the problem. Now there's the rub.
Do I listen, speak, go soak in the tub?
Saw ourselves as Commander-in-Chief, Moralist,
Know-it-all, Judge, Critic, Amateur Psychologist.
We learned Reflective Listening and practiced that night.
Open, not closed responses, so we could do it with might.

Step six; You-Messages blame, criticize, accuse.
I-Messages express feelings and concerns. They're great to use.
Instead of shouting, You're late, you're grounded, go to bed.
State, When you're late, I worry you've had
an accident, hurt your head.
Brainstorming a problem for a plan to make,
Gives teens a stake in solution, less likely rules to break.

Step seven; Reward and Punishment are replaced,
Natural or logical consequences faced.

Step eight; Match disciplinary approach to behavior of teen.
This step combines all we've learned. Got to be keen.

Step nine; Equality and democracy are best kept in tow.
By the Family Meeting, why not give it a go.

So step right up, step right this way.
We're ready to take on our teen today.
And thank you, Jeanne, for your help and time
And inspiration for this rhyme.

Thank you for your willingness to lend a listening ear,
To help, advise, a young life to steer.
For understanding of problems big and small,
Your genuine concern no matter the call.
Your spiritual guidance when asked what to do,
Your prayers for direction that helped, too.
Your honest approach, with love and care your tools,
Makes Jeanne the *Guardian Angel of Waubonsie Valley High School.*

Tribute to Jeanne Tiffany, High School Counselor, May 6, 1990.

Jeanne, at only seventy-two years of age,
died from the coronavirus, on
April 9, 2020

Farewell

A farewell poem, written for you. From each one of us, too.

Koenekamps will miss you all right.
Who'll their boys play with day and night?
Brenda and Steve and Michael and Scott,
Hate you leaving, they'll miss you a lot.

Potters will miss seeing skateboards each day,
The kids playing in their own special way.
Ron, who likes to jump bikes with the boys.
Is going to miss their special toys.

Hesses will miss you and your pets.
Good luck moving, finding a vet.
Animal lovers, Jerry and Sandy,
Going to miss your Susie and Brandy.

Van Arysdales hate to see you go.
No Christmas lights, not the same show.
Bonnie, Sara, Rachael, Jim, and all,
Will miss those street games with bat and ball.

Sharpes will miss you when you move away.
Brent and Chad like to watch you boys play
Soccer games and scoring, in the street,
Seven-Eleven store candy to eat.

Phillips say farewell, to the east coast you go.
Mike, Polly, Crystal, hope you have sunshine, no snow.
We'll all miss those cute smiles on your faces.
When you move away to your new places

And when you are moved, all settled in,
Sit back, remember us with a grin.
Fun years, your little boys were growing,
And all the Dads were outside mowing.

Children were always in the street,
Something to play, something to eat
Your boat and all your water fun,
Deer Spring Place, California sun.
And just because you move away,
Doesn't mean you can't come back for a stay.
Health, happiness, and love to you.
May all your hopes and dreams come true.

We'll miss you, so keep in touch.
Send a photo, write a bunch.
Good luck, good wishes from us all.
Take on Virginia, have a ball.
1985

Karen's Guest Book Tribute

Friends for always, you and me.
Friends for always, since 1990.
Talking, laughing, helping do,
Shopping, walking, biking, too.
Sharing, caring, always there.
Hopes, dreams, and problems to share.

Forever alike in many ways.
Forever catching up on our days.
Husbands, children, our family life,
Marriages, moving, everyday strife.
There isn't anything we can't share.
Together, there isn't anything we can't bear.

Old memories shared from our past.
New memories made that will last.
Dinner, Bread Pudding at Long Island Cafe.
Tracking the UPS truck to Ron's dismay.
Relaxing in hot tub or by pool out back.
Your Southern Hospitality, nothing to lack.
Closet organizing, donations for Cuba cause.
Did talking ever wear out our jaws?

Outfits planned for upcoming events,
So we can impress our special gents.
Sharing Coconut Cream Pie at Laura Albert's diner.
Good friends talking, what could be finer.
Drinks in the bar, unusual Husk dinner.
Chocolates and candy always a winner.

Family Circle Cup with a snack of Kettle Korn,
Pam Shriver's autograph, your hat will adorn.
Music, candles, movies, and wine.
Unforgettable tennis time.

We weren't born into the same family,
But sisters we will always be.
Thank you for sharing your time and space,
In your Isle of Palms special place.
April 2014

Basia, our Exercising Expert

We heard someone is celebrating the big seven oh.
We are especially grateful that this person lives here in the HO.
We want to say happy birthday to you.
May all your dreams and hopes come true.
We hope you don't run out of toilet paper, too.
We are blessed that you are our fitness guru.

Thank you, our exercising expert, dear Basia,
For leading us in Yoga Ashtanga.
The coronavirus has caused your exercising friends much distress,
Your classes have given us peace and rest.

Cleansing breaths help release the tension,
Cleansing breaths help us focus on our intention.
Sun Salutations with hands to our toes,
Trying to breathe, to our knees, touch our nose.

Up Dog and Down Dog, Chaturanga,
Five breaths, then a smooth Vinyasa.
Carefully coming into a pose called Chair,
Sit on pretend toilet, see toes, arms raised, if you dare.

How low can you go in your Warrior Pose II?
Gaze to your straight arm, inhale life anew.
For the Twist, to our left then twist to our right,
Look over shoulder, bind with all might.

For balance, we practice Tree Pose,
Seeing how high off the mat, we can lift our leg and toes.
Bridge Up to open chest, strengthen back,

Be careful as your vertebrae you stack.
Knees to chest rolling side to side,
On our mats, lying down, we just want to abide.
Final stretching, closing poses,
Shoulder stand, Plow, Fish, breathing through our noses.

Total relaxation, blue sky above, palm trees sway,
Mockingbird mocking, water ripple sounds, perfect day.
Basia ends yoga saying, *Thank you for doing your practice with me.*
My Light bows to Your Light for all to see. Namaste.
But wait, Basia is not through.
On other days, this is what we do:
Warm-ups and weights, we exercise all body parts
To strengthen our muscles, cardio for our hearts.

We strengthen gluts, quads, pecs, triceps,
Hamstrings, four shoulder muscles, and biceps.
We do sit-ups called *Basia's Bitches*
So our tummies and tushes fit into our britches.

We do special exercises for our legs, hips, thighs,
Lunges, squats, kicks, lift knees high.
We work all muscle groups untill we moan,
Then stretch and are happy to feel toned.

The best part about gathering at pool side,
Cordial, caring, companionship, and faithful friendships abide.
Love,
Brenda F., Brenda S., Donna, Karen, Linda, Lynn, Pat

During COVID-19 quarantine, friends met at our neighborhood pool,
standing six feet apart, for exercising classes led by our friend Basia,
a fitness instructor. What a blessing to be able to continue staying
fit during challenging times.

My Dallas Angel

I met Linda Trimmer on the phone one day.
She was helping my sister, Connie, in her dismay.
Parkinson's disease, dementia, depression, a critical crisis,
Linda was there to lend a helping hand. Priceless.

Her friendship and Christian connection over the years
Would be put to hard tests, rejections from Connie she feared.
Linda met me at the Dallas Airport in her shorts and T-shirt attire.
Genuinely caring and kind, to help Connie she did aspire.

We quickly became attached in spirit and mind
As over the next years we would find,
Working together we made a great team,
Even when situations were impossible, it did seem.

Linda was *the boots on the Dallas ground*,
Many a mile she would pound
Making hospital visits, trips to help Josh,
Searching for care facilities, figuring out the chaos.

Hours on the phone interviewing, asking questions.
Hours on the phone, making helpful suggestions.
Together we made it through the hospital stay,
And Josh's wanting to keep away.

Shopping with Josh to help him regain
Independence, a feeling he could be sane.
Shopping with Josh for Connie's needs.
She was always there, helping indeed.

Three months at Brookhaven Nursing Care,
Atria's invite for Connie to move there and then a no-go, how dare.

Then finally, an answer to prayer,
Mary Ann and close by Memory Care.

Wyndham facility discovery.
Perfect for our Miss Connie.
Who is this woman who so freely gives?
Who is this woman who so freely lives?

She is not a Dallas Cowboy Cheerleader
But she is my Dallas Cowgirl, angel, cheer giver.
I hope she knows how very much I need her!

We share the same name, I know it was meant to be.
God put her into my life just to help me see
The uncharted path to bring aid to my sister,
My husband's health needs, even though I missed her.

Linda was there when I could not be!
I will always be grateful, I hope you see.

Lovingly,
Linda Potter
April 11, 2020

I reside in Sarasota with my husband who had eight surgeries in a year.

A large part of my time was spent caring for my husband. My sister lived in Dallas and was struggling with Parkinson's disease and other serious health issues. Caring for my sister long distance was a difficult task. Linda, my Dallas Angel, helped make it all work. Linda is an amazing friend, good-hearted soul, and a beautiful lady. Every time she helped my sister, I smiled. She told me no one had ever written a poem about her. Glad I made her smile.

Namaste

Thank you Yoga instructors, Lauren and Mary,
For Yoga breathing,
And new ways we are now believing.
For your love and care and healing Reiki ways,
Your smile and patience on teaching days.

For Up Dog and Down Dog and Chaturanga,
High Lunge, Low Lunge and safe Vinyasa.
For Warrior Poses and Sun Salutations,
Restful Child's Pose and different Plank positions.
For Tiangle, Bridging Up, Chair Pose, and Side Plank.
We now breathe to keep our minds blank.

Yoga has:
Boosted our moods and confidence.
Improved flexibility and overall balance.
Lowered blood pressure and reduced inflammation.
Slowed the aging process and increased relaxation.

Strengthened muscles and overall brain health.
Just breathe, breathe, breathe for an improved image of self.
Yoga has become an important part
Of our exercise routine and how our days start.

You've touched our souls and changed our hearts
And helped us stay sweet instead of tart.
Your closing remarks have inspired us to be
Better women for the world to see.
You are our guru authority!

My First Step

Glad your taste buds approved the zucchini bread treat.
It was exciting for me to meet and greet.

Delicious, healthy salad for lunch.
That we would be friends, a correct hunch.

Your condo is beautiful beyond measure.
The entire day a pure pleasure.

The poem you sent was very clever.
Encouraging to know a bright mentor.

Hugs,
Linda Potter
Poet
October 23, 2019

Meeting Barbara Feltquate was the first step in my publishing journey. During our lunch meeting, Barbara walked me through the publishing process, encouraged me and insisted on my perseverance. Her published books were beautifully presented. She gave me her publisher, provided valuable information, was available for questions with answers, and made me believe I was a true poet.

Retyping most of my poems into my current computer files seemed like an impossible task. When would I have time for all the work involved? Then the coronavirus forced all to stay at home. Suddenly, I had time to start typing. Past memories, from my poems, flooded my days, as my husband and I relived many fond events in our incredibly blessed life. Typing my poems was excellent therapy and kept me positive during a most difficult and scary time.